Y0-BRH-707

TRAFFICKING IN WOMEN AND CHILDREN IN INDIA

JOINT WOMEN'S PROGRAMME PUBLICATIONS

Status of Rural Women in India	75.00
Status of Nurses in India	60.00
Status of Single Women in India	125.00
Status of Women in Quran (Urdu)	05.00
Good News for Women (Bible Study)	05.00
(English, Tamil, Kannada, Telegu, Bengali and Hindi)	
Women in Organised Movements	45.00
Women in Praise and Struggle (Bible Study)	05.00
Vision and Service (Bible Study)	10.00
(English and Hindi)	
Women and Law	05.00
The Problem of Dowry in Bangalore City	05.00
The Devadasi Problem (English and Kannada)	05.00
Indian Women in Media	12.00
Changes in Christian Personal Laws	03.50
Child Labour in Bangalore City	30.00
The Women's Decade 1975-85, An Assessment	30.00
The Basavi Cult	05.00
Women in the CNI Diocese of Delhi	05.00
Pavement Dwellers in Calcutta	15.00
Christian Marriage and Customary Practices in Manipur	15.00

Status of Women Series

TRAFFICKING IN WOMEN
AND
CHILDREN IN INDIA

(Sexual Exploitation and Sale)

Sr. M. Rita Rozario R.G.S.

Assisted by

Mr Javed Rasool
Mr Pradeep Kesari

A Joint Women's Programme Publication

UPPAL PUBLISHING HOUSE
New Delhi—110002

UPPAL PUBLISHING HOUSE
3, Ansari Road, Daryaganj, New Delhi-110002

For

William Carey Study and Research Centre
14/2 Sudder Street, Calcutta 700 016
and
Joint Women's Programme

ⓒWilliam Carey Study and Research Centre
1988

ISBN 81-85024—34—0

Printed in India
Published by UPPAL PUBLISHING HOUSE
3, Ansari Road, Daryaganj, New Delhi 110002
and Printed at Bharat Enterprises Delhi-1100053

Dedicated to

Dedicated to the Victims of Sexual Exploitation

"Friend, I speak on behalf of
the victimized, the trapped, the harassed, the branded,
the mutilated, the tortured the moulded—shaped to suit
the lust of sexual exploiters . . . .

They are human like you and me
persons with body, mind and soul
born to live with human dignity
...   .
They are human like you and me"

From a poem by Sr. Rita

FOREWORD

This study, "Trafficking in Women and Children in India", is a culmination of several other studies that have been done by the JWP on the various aspects of the problem of prostitution. The first was "The Devadasi Problem" which enabled the Karnataka government to draft and finally pass the bill on "The Karnataka (Devadasi Prohibition of Dedication) Act 1981." The second was "The Basavi Cult in Andhra Pradesh," and the third a general study of different types of Prostitution in West Bengal, Tamil Nadu, Andhra Pradesh, Uttar Pradesh and Karnataka.

The present study, however, was designed to bring to light the mechanism through which helpless girls are trapped into the night-marish world of prostitution. It proves our point that poverty alone is not the root cause of prostitution. It is coupled with the existing socio-religious status of women and the prevailing caste structure. It has also proved my statement that the majority of girls in prostitution are forced into this practice by unscrupulous people, poor parents and guardians, and other social pressures. What needs to be considered when framing a suitable legislation is that women alone cannot be blamed, but society and its attitude towards women, the clients who demand prostitutes, the procurers who kidnap, sell and buy girls, and the pimps who act as go-betweens should also be held responsible.

This is no ordinary study of a problem that is as old as history it self. It is a labour of love by a woman who has found herself deeply involved in the lives of prostitutes at first hand. The suffering of the women and children became her suffering, the problem of sexual exploitation became more the deeper she delved into it. Sister Rita could not treat the never ending 'cases' as mere statistics. Each was a haman life that had somehow 'missed the mark,' as she put it; missed the opportunity of becoming fully human.

The total involvement of the author in her work has meant that editors have had to cut down her material. But I hope that the message of the main findings will come through loud and clear—that in India sexual exploitation usually starts in childhood and quite often it is the children's own relatives who are responsible for it.

I commend this book to sociologists as well as concerned laymen and laywomen with the hope that it will awaken society to attend to one of its most hidden and most degrading problems.

JYOTSNA CHATTERJI

Associate Director

W C S R C

Incharge of Joint Women's Programme

PREFACE

After centuries of lethargy and submission to the status quo, more and more women have roused themselves and want to know why and how they have become subjected to male rule and what can be done about it. However, when they go in search of explanation they discover to their dismay how little information is available on subjects of utmost concern to half the population of India—the women. History has been written primarily from the standpoint of men.

The Joint Women's Programme of WCSRC—CISRS, from its inception was aware of this situation. It had committed itself to study and action. It had several publications to its credit—'Rape,' 'Dowry,' 'Discrimination in Laws,' (in employment. wages, etc.)—topics related to women's concerns.

In 1981, Joint Women's Programme undertook a study on the 'Devadasis of North Karnataka.' This book received a wide press coverage and publicity. A follow up meeting with the Devadasis brought to light the need for a study on prostituttion. Accordingly in 1982, a study on prostitution was conducted. This further highlighted the need for an in-depth study at a more comprehensive level to be undertaken in the area of Sexual Exploitation and Sale of Women and Children in India (1983). (JWP had already made a study on the Basavi Cult in Andhra Pradesh. This practice is similar to the Devadasi practice.)

The year 1973 marked a new phase in the annals of the Good Shepherd Sisters in India. Sr. M. Francis Xavier Collins (Provincial) opened a Diagnostic-cum-Reception Centre for screening applicants seeking placement in Good Shepherd Orphanages, Protective and Rescue Homes, in India.

Service at this Centre brought the researcher in direct contact with the victims and some victimizers of flesh-trade. In the past the focus was on rescue and rehabilitation of the victims. Institutions in general served the victims and did not reach out to the victimizers.

The researcher was convinced that while serving the victims, she could not ignore the victimizers; while extending rescue and rehabilitative services, she could not omit the preventive aspect; while attending to the visible—the tip of the iceburg—the symptom, she could not over look the invisible, the root cause of the evil, the malady. She was aware that the solution to this problem could not be sought in isolation but ought to be taken up in the context of the whole situation that exists in our society in India. At this juncture (mid 1983) the researcher met Mrs. Chatterji, Associate Director of the Joint Women's Programme at a meeting. They both expressed the need for an in-depth study of Sexual Exploitation and the Sale of Women and Children and Mrs. Chatterji requested the researcher to undertake the study.

In 1983, the Good Shepherd Sisters in India, realising the complexity of the problems faced by women and children, resolved to release the researcher for the purpose of this study. And so slowly but surely this study came to be written.

SR.M. RITA ROZARIO

ACKNOWLEDGEMENTS

I wish to place on record my deep K. Chatterji, Professor Saral gratitude to Director—WCSRC—CISRS, and Ms. Jyotsna Chatterji, Associate Director—JWP, for initiating this study, for their continued support and above all for their steadfast commitment to the cause undertaken—without which it would have been impossible for me to complete this study.

My special thanks to late Sr. Peter Jacinto (Generalate) for her keen interest and encouragement given to undertake the present study. My sincere thanks to Sr. Mercy Abhrahim (Provicial) and her Councillors for releasing me for this study.

I would like to take this opportunity to express my deep gratitude for the services extended by several persons, organisations and institutions in India—in particular I would like to mention the names of the following:

Sri Garudachar	—Director General and Inspector General of Police, Karnataka.
Sri Malliah	—Director General of Prisons.
Sri P.G. Harlankar	—Commissioner of Police, Bangalore, Karnataka.
Sri J.F. Ribeiro	—Commissioner of Police, Greater Bombay, Maharashtra.
Sri K. Mohan Das	—Director General (Intelligence) Tamil Nadu.

Sri Kadam & Officials (Police)	—Vigilance/Crime Branch, Greater Bombay Maharashtra.
Superintendents, Officials (Police)	—Karnataka State.
Mrs. Veena Rao	—Deputy Commissioner of Bellary.
Officials (Vigilance Branch)	—Madras—Tamil Nadu.
Dr. H.M. Marulasiddaiah	—Head of the Department—Social Work—Bangalore University.
Dr. K.N. George (Director) Dr. Jaya Singh (Asst. Director)	The Madras School of Social Work, Egmore T.N.
Dr. Dorothy M. Baker Dr. Hazel D'lima	—Nirmala Niketan, College of Social Work, Bombay.
Ms. Radha Paul & Faculty	—Department of Social Work, Stella Maris, Madras.
Ms. Rabia Yusuf	—Additional Director, Directorate of Women and Children's Welfare, Bangalore.
Ms. Padma Mehta	—Deputy Director Correctional Administration, Directorate of Women and Child Welfare, Pune, Maharashtra.
Ms. Tara Cherian	—Chairperson State Social Welfare Board Nandanam, Madras, T.N.
Ms. Shakuntala Lall	—Association of Social Health in India—New Delhi.
Superintendents & Staff	—Government State Homes, Karnataka. Protective Home, Chembur Bombay Asha Sadam, Umerkhadi, Bombay Sukh Shanti, Chembur, Bombay Arulagam, Madurai, Tamil Nadu.

I acknowlede with gratitude the help received from the victims and victimizers of the flesh-trade. In spite of risks involved to their lives, they co-operated with us. Through their kindness we were led to a better understanding of this problem.

My appreciation and thanks to all those who have helped me in data collection, sharing the data collecting, interpreting, translating, typing, etc. In this regard I would like to mention Vincent A. Xavier, Javed Rasool, Pradeep Kesari, K.J. Prasad, J. Sarala, R. Nirmala Susheela, R.S. Purushotham, S.K. Basu Mallik and Mr. Somnath Chakravorthy, Sheela Barse and Sandhya Sharma, the staff JWP and CISRS, India.

My deep gratitute to Dr. Shantha Mohan for her patient guiding, to the 30 experts in India for their constructive criticism on the interview schedule, to Mrs. Jane Caleb, Mrs. Chatterji for meticulously attending to every detail and editing this book.

Last, but not least, my sincere gratitude to the members, of my family (Rozarios) for assisting me in innumerable ways and for having stood by me in my difficulties encountered during this study.

SR. RITA ROZARIO

CONTENTS

LIST OF TABLES

LIST OF SKETCHES

Patterns of Trafficking

1

INTRODUCTION

The Right to be Human

Recent newspaper articles, magazines and films have lifted the curtain on the underworld of sexual exploitation in India today —and particularly on the sale of young girls for prostitution. But these media have only been able to give a glimpse of a whole institution which is extremely complex and reinforced by age-old historical and religious attitudes as well as modern day consumerism, tourism and migration patterns.

This book, therefore, aims to give the reader a wider understanding of the whole nature of the problem of prostitution. The field study, which took nearly four years, will give details on how the institution of prostitution is sustained and perpetuated. The other chapters, which are equally important, will go deeper and examine the cultural and historical roots of the problem in the low status of women and the misunderstanding, or deliberate abuse, of the true nature of human sexuality.

Persons, human beings, are relational beings with the capacity for entering into partnership with God and each other. It is this relational capacity which distinguishes human life from other forms of created life and which bestows upon human life its unique worth. Thus the fundamental worth of human life is not rooted in the amount of wisdom or wealth which a person possesses, or in the degree to which a person is regarded as a useful member of society.

Persons are beings with numerous possibilities—beings-on-the-way—who actuate themselves consciously and critically and interact with their surrounding world.

Occasionally people say that 'human rights' include the right to earn one's living in whatever way one wishes, including prostitution, and they advocate legalization of prostitution. But human rights are rooted in a vision, a concept and a notion of what it is to be human. Being human cannot be reduced to or defined in terms of human rights that have been set down in legal codes. Being human is far more all-embracing than legal codes of right. The 'right to be human' must be enshrined in human rights. By virtue of being born a human being with inherent dignity and equal and inalienable rights every person is entitled to live in freedom, justice and peace.

Whenever the dominant stream becomes inhuman and intolerable for the rest of the society, there has been significant protest movements upholding the value of the person and human dignity.

Prostitution is devoid of truthful love, genuine relationship, respect to persons. Protection against destruction and exploitation is the hall mark of respect to persons. This is totally absent in sexual exploitation and sale.

Organisation of Sexual Relations in Society

Social anthropologists state that promiscuity proceeded marriage and family. Primitive economy in its evolutionary process gave birth to higher forms of production. This was made possible by the use of axe and other handmade tools, in utilising the land and water resources, to productivity. Improved production not only required improved tools but also better organisation of social labour and distribution of the product. The concept of property was born and it transformed the existing social relations. Sex behaviour had to be controlled and defined and marriage was institutionalised.

The adoption of polyandrous marriage might have been due to a preponderance of males matched by a lesser proportion of females. Likewise, demand for women with the lesser supply of men, reflecting the sex gap in social composition among other things might have led to polygamous marriages.

Marriage by forcible abduction can be traced as early as 2500 BC—1500 BC in Rig Veda. The hilly-Himalayan tract occupies a place of special significance in the annals of anthropology for the cultural practice of fraternal polyandry.

The need for social organisation of sexual relations in human beings was felt by civilized societies on the strong belief that outside marriage they adversely disturb the stability of the family. (Besides being destructive and degrading to the participating individuals). Ever since marriage received abiding recognition as a necessary social institution, sex outside matrimony was considered a threat to monogamous morality.

Man in his greed to gain larger and larger territory and wealth, not only conquered kingdoms but also men and women. The prisoners of war were brought to the native land and the women were enslaved. The enslaved women were forced into prostitution. For example in Greece enslaved women were subjected to purchase and sale and traffic in them was permitted by licensing the prostitutes in brothels.

A woman was purchased and possessed; her sexual favours were demanded; her birthpangs produced children; her labour yielded profit in agricultural production and finally after the birth of the children she was disposed of to avoid further expense on her.

Thus the reduction of women and children from human persons to just bodies, objects for male utility and disposal was enforced and it continues even today by means of a vast net work of control ranging from the most subtle to the most brutal. The most glaring form of this control, is the sexual exploitation of women and children in sale and prostitution.

Like slavery in the usual sense, prostitution has an economic aspect while being a cultural phenomenon rooted in the masculine and feminine images given currency by society; it is a market and indeed a very lucrative one. The merchandise is unfortunately supplied by physical intimacy with women and children. Thus the alienation of the person is here more far reaching than in slavery in its usual sense, where what is alienated is working strength not intimacy; it is a betrayal of truthful love—sexual exploitation.

2

HISTORICAL PERSPECTIVE ON
PROSTITUTION

India has a long recorded history and great store is set by tradition. Therefore, it is important to trace the history of prostitution and the sale of women to see how far practices in the past account for the position of women in present day society and reinforce toleration of assaults on the dignity of women by sexual violence and forced prostitution.

The evidence from the remote period of Indian history indicates that prostitution was an accepted profession to which were attached certain prerogatives, rights and duties (Henriques, Fernando 1961. 142).

During the Brahamana period the prostitutes were called Veshya and it is conjectured that they were created to minister to the *Vish* or traders and merchants who led a life cut off from home and wives. (Basu and Sinha 1929:22,28). It seems that it was from Egypt that legal prostitution found its way into India. The prostitutes were variously known as *ganika, bandhaki rupajiva, veshya, varangana, Kultani, sambhali, pumscali*, etc.

In the sacred books of the Hindus, including the Ramayana and the Mahabharata, there are frequent references to prostitution. The kings when they returned to their kingdom were received by an escort of honour consisting of armies and *ganikas* (Mbh. V 86, 15, 16: XIII 53: 66; Ram VI 127, 3, Mbh IV 68.24, 29. CD Arthasastra. Book I Ch 27 Sutra 123-124).

Marriage with the prostitute was not looked down upon. The great sage, Vasista, for example, was the son of a woman engaged in prostitution (Vajrasuchi Upanishad). The dancing girls were part of the court and were called *rajavarishyas* (royal prostitutes).

The great epics besides giving an account of the high status and privileges that the *ganikas* and courtesans enjoyed at this time, also relate that degeneration had set in. The prostitutes followed in the expeditions of the kings (Ram II 36, 2-3; Mhb III 239, 22-24) and accompanied armies in the battle-field (Mhb V 195, 19). This implies that women prostitutes could be taken wherever the male wanted for his pleasure and even exposed to the dangers of war. They had become commodities and were taken to the battle-field to satisfy the sexual desires of the soldiers.

The stern law givers of the epic age no doubt tried to keep a check, but the popular trend seems to have gone on even in the teeth of regulations.

During the Buddhist Period, in spite of the adverse public opinion and punishments, courtesans existed. The Jataka (315, 481) gives an interesting description of the economic conditions that prevailed in Kali's brothel.

Although prostitution was looked down upon by Jainism, no special stigma seems to have been attached to it. According to Jain sources, prostitution was so rampant in the country that Jain nuns were cautioned against it.

Greek writers (326 BC) state that on the eve of Alexander's invasion some of the Indians exposed their daughters for sale in the open market. The deterioration of society and the social conditions can be well imagined. During Chandra Gupta Mauriya's time (324-300 BC) the Greek envoy Megasthenes wrote that Amazons guarded the Emperor's harem and formed the main bodyguard of the king. These women acted as a security force for the personal safety of the king. They were also efficient in the intelligence service of the king.

Patliputra was at this time the flourishing centre of prostitution, and it was probably for the first time the attention of the state was drawn to a colony of prostitutes for its effective control and to bring it under the obligation of a stabilized taxation (Basu and Sinha 1933:202). The evidence of prostitution at this period comes from Kautilya who wrote *Arthasastra*, (321-296 BC). He used words such as *ganikas, praganiha, dasi, devadasi, rupadasi*, etc., for coutesans and prostitutes (Chandra Mati: 1976:64).

During Ashoka's reign (272-232 BC) the superintendents of the royal harem and the courtesans were called Shri-Adhyaksha Mahamattas, and their posts were maintained most likely till the seventh century AD.

Kamasutra Vatsayayana, written probably in the early centuries of the Christian era, is the most important source of information about courtesans and prostitutes in ancient India. He systematized a considerable amount of floating material about courtesans . . . . . The sixth chapter of *Kamasutra* deals exclusively with courtesans. The work deals with all aspects of love and inevitably there is a section on prostitution. In Vatsayayana's classification the lowest type was the *Kumbhadasi* or common harlots. They used to entertain anyone who could afford their low price. A *Kulata* was a married woman who practised prostitution. A *Paricharika* or attendant, was the daughter of a courtesan who went through a form of brothel marriage. Her marriage contract allowed her to perform prostitution but her husband was to be preferred to the clients.

Shillapadikaram, written between 2nd and 5th century AD gives details of courtesans in South India.

When Harsha ascended the throne (622 AD approximately). the traditional freedom and patronage of the dancing girls continued.

Kuvalayamala, written in 779 AD by Udyotanasuti at Jalvd in Rajasthan, is one of the books that gives a glimpse of courtesans of the Medieval times.

The system of attaching prostitutes to places of worship is of ancient origin, but it seems to have come into regular practice during the ninth and tenth centuries when the ritual in the temples attained the present form.

The destruction of great temples by Muslim invaders and erection of Mosques in the place of temples was the beginning of the decline of the devadasi system in North India. But in South India, which was ruled by the Hindu Rajas, the institution flourished with the same vigour as it did in pre-Muslim India.

Vijayanagar Empire (1336-1565 AD) at the zenith of its glory conferred considerable social recognition on the devadasis. (Patil, B.R.: 1975:378). From Elliot's work on History of India, we get a clear description of prostitution in Vijayanagar Kingdom. He describes it as follows:

> "Behind the mint there is a sort of bazar which is more than 300 yards long and 20 yards broad . . . and anyone who passes through this place makes choice of whom he wishes. The servants of these brothels take care of whatever is taken into them, and if anything is lost they are dismissed. There are several brothels within these seven fortresses and the revenues from them, which as stated before amount to 12,000 fanams, go to pay the wages of the policemen". (Elliot, H.M.: Vol IV: 1867-1877; 111-112).

The rulers who followed Krishnadeva Raya were incompetent with the result Vijayanagar gradually declined in power. Polygamy, sati and child marriages were common.

In the Mughal Period (1526-1787 AD) prostitution was a recognised institution, but among Muslims prostitution was the antithesis to the institution of family life, and while the singing and dancing girls who practised it became rich and even powerful, they were never treated as part of society, as they had been in earlier times.

Emperor Akbar (1556-1605 AD) made some regulations so that the service of the prostitutes might not be available very easily to the public. Prostitutes were confined to a place out-side the capital city. This place was known as *Shaitanpura* or the devil's quarters.

From Badaoni's and Abdul Fazl's description we come to know that Akbar privately called a number of well-known prostitutes of the city, and asked them to disclose the names of the persons who seduced them. The Amirs who had seduced them were reprimanded and severely punished. (Abdul Fazl, about 1590 AD-301).

Emperor Shahjahan (1627-1657 AD) reviewed the activities once again. When Aurangzeb became the ruler, most of his rules were directed towards prohibition of prostitution,

In spite of the many regulations imposed by the Mughal emperors like Akbar and Aurangzeb, prostitution received great encouragement from the rich and well-to-do sections of the people.

Not only the Mughal rulers, but also the Hindu Rajas like Baz Bahadur, the ruler of Malwa, and Raja Indrajit Singh, the ruler of Orchha State in Rajasthan, were great patrons of prostitution.

The coming of the European Power (in the 15th century) to India, especially the English, played an important role in bringing about the downfall of the Mughal Empire. They discouraged the sati system, class hatred, child marriage, purdah system. Female education and re-marriage of widows were encouraged. Laws dealing with immoral traffic were enacted under British rule. However, in many provinces official police registers were kept, for the convenience of the police "to keep an eye on the anti-social elements who usually frequented the brothels." It was in 1923 that the Suppression of Immoral Traffic Act (SIT Act) was passed for Calcutta. Madras and Bombay Presidencies followed suit. In U.P., the Nayak Girls' Protection Act and Minor Girls' Protection Act were passed in 1923. Attempts at abolition of brothels began after the passing of these Acts.

After Independence, more systematic attention has been paid to this problem. Both preventive and curative aspects of the problem have been taken up for policy formulation and implementation. Appointment of the Committee known as the Advisory Committee on Social and Moral Hygiene was set up by the Central Social and Welfare Board as early as in 1954. There was some awakening among the leading social workers and reformers. This Advisory Committee toured different states. They interviewed magistrates, police officials, lawyers, doctors and social workers. They visited the institutions housing destitute women. Their field coverage was extensive—86 towns and over 100 institutions in all states excepts Manipur, Tripura and Kutch, were included.

The report of the Committee brings out forcefully some characteristic features of this profession. It says, "Prostitution existed in every state of India except Coorg. The brothels are often situated on important streets in cities. There is nothing clandestine about the display of the prostitutes. In cities like Bombay where brothels are illegal, a brothel system exists in a camourflaged form, so that prostitutes who practise quite openly, can get behind the law. . . They have all single room tenements and carry on this nefarious trade as independent individuals (Raghuramaiah K. Laxmi, "Law and Immoral Traffic", in Joshi and Bhatia (eds) *Readings in Social Defence*, 1981.

The Suppression of Immoral Traffic in Women and Girls Act (SIT Act) was passed by Parliament in 1956 and amended in 1986 as the Prevention of Immoral Traffic in Women and Girls. Let us look at the extent of prostitution in India as exposed by the SIT Act.

Under the SIT Act there were in all 4,173 cases in 1966. In 1968, this figure reached 7,295. In 1970 only 6,738 cases were reported under this Act. In that year cases from U.P. and Jammu and Kashmir were not included in the list. The state-wise number of cases under prostitution in 1970 was as follows: Andhra Pradesh 1,936; Maharashtra 268, Mysore 1,678; Tamil Nadu 2,703. The remaining 14 states had in all 85 cases. From West Bengal only 20 cases were reported during 1970. In seven union territories there were 68 cases. They were all from one place: Union Territory of Delhi. Out of 6,738 cases, as many as 1,380 or over one fifth were from eight large cities. The name of the city and prostitution cases were as follows:

Hyderabad 639, Bangalore 497, Bombay 101, Delhi 68, Madras 31, Kanpur 23, Calcutta 20 and Ahmedabad 1. The conviction rate is usually above 90 per cent. In 1970, a total of 6,540 cases were investigated under SIT Act. Of them 6,292 (94 per cent) were convicted. Only 248 were acquitted or let off. In 1973, as many as 11,816 cases were filed. During the seven year period (1966-1973), there was a three fold rise in the incidence of prostitution as revealed by official statistics on prostitution. (Government of India, *Crime in India* 1970. Bureau of Police Research and Development, 1972. Also see Ministry of Education and Social Welfare, *Handbook on Social Welfare Services*, Government of India, 1976).

Official Statistics are reported under special and local laws declared to be cognisable. It is not a complete picture on the extent of prostitution in India. For that matter, no one really knows the exact situation.

Kate Millet, a legal aid in America, writes: "The actual situation in the city is that prostitution is accepted by everyone the police, judge, clerk and lawyers. Arrest and prosecution are purely gestures that have to be made to keep up the facade of public morality. The method of dealing with it is simply a form of harassment not a form of prevention, abolition or punishment. . . . only a total and satisfied acceptance of the double standard, excusing the male, accusing the female". (Millet Kate, *The Prostitution Papers*, 1971. (Quoted in Mary Gibson, *op. cit.*)

What is the situation in India with regard to prostitution in the 1980s?

Today licensing and legalising prostitution in India is a controversial issue. The signs of this debate are surfacing in social welfare organisations, in government circles and in certain women's organisations.

The current of thought advocating legalisation, that is prevalent among certain welfare organisations, the police and government circle's argued that (a) prostitution is a necessary social evil which exists because of man's sexual appetite, sexual agressiveness and polygamous behaviour which is natural and biological (b) prostitution is a safety valve for the maintenance

of the family structure (c) prostitution prevents rampant rape
(d) a prostitute is a major source of Sexually Transmitted
Deseases. Registration of prostitution, segregation and treatment of prostitutes would control STD (e) since the Suppression
of Immoral Traffic in Women and Girls Act 1956 (SIT Act) has
not controlled prostitution, legalisation is necessary.

Legalisation of prostitution is advocated on the grounds
that (a) often it is a woman's choice and she has full control
of her body and sexuality, (b) it is a profession like any other.
If a woman can sell her intellectual and manual skills, why not
her body? (c) since prostitution cannot be presently eliminated
from our sexist society, legislation accompanied by demands
for ending police harassment and the introduction of minimum
wages, creches for their children, better living conditions and
health facilities, would afford some measure of protection for
prostitutes (d) legislation would wipe out the stigma of immorality and criminality.

The opponents of these theories strongly object to legislation
of prostitution in India on the grounds that:

(a) Segregation, medical treatment will not be able to
    control STD as prostitutes are not the only source of
    STD;

(b) Registration and legalisation would destroy a woman's
    private identity; she would be considered as a public
    woman;

(c) Accepting and legitimising prostitution would mean
    women's bodies are commodities, thus making them the
    public property of several males who can purchase her
    for a price;

(d) These women labelled and ostracised and at the same
    time sought after as safety-valves, would reflect the
    double standards of society.

Already Ujjain Municipal Corporation in a notification has
now asked all prostitutes operating within its areas to pay an

annual licence fee of Rs. 50 each and furnish medical certificates from the District Medical Officer with attested photographs.

Of late, both Central and a few State Governments have shown signs of wavering. India is a signatory to the New York Convention of 1950!

Words of Gandhiji, the Father of the Nation, are worth quoting here:

> "It is a matter of bitter shame and sorrow and of deep humiliation that a number of women have to sell their chastity for men's lust. Man the law-giver will have to pay a dreadful penalty for the degradation he had imposed upon the so-called weaker sex. When woman freed from man's snares rises to the full height and rebels against man's legis- lation and institution designed by him, her rebellion, no doubt non-violent, will be none the less effective." (Report of the Fifth All India Conference on Moral and Social Hygiene, 1956, p. 24).

3

THE IMPACT OF RELIGION ON THE STATUS OF WOMEN

In sexual exploitation and sale of women and children—which includes prostitution—we find persons are denied their right to be human. Why is it so? This question cannot be brushed aside or ignored. It must be faced and honestly met. Upon its answer hinges the whole question of either the eradication or the sustaining of sexual exploitation, including prostitution and sale.

Are women and children considered as human beings, full persons in their own right, in India?

This is the question that must be first considered and finally answered. A study of the religions of India may help us here as religions have played a major role in moulding the life of men and women throughout the ages.

The basic purpose behind all religious teachings, and the common quest of all religious masters was the 'quality of life of man' and how man can improve the quality of human existence. All religions tell their people how they should organise their life and relationships—both private and public—if they want to achieve the quality of life pointed out by them. All religious leaders give reasons for the miseries experienced by man in his life and how to eliminate them. That is why they were listened to, obeyed and even worshipped by people.

Strangely enough, at the dawn of the great ancient cultures of the Middle East, it was female divinities that ruled heaven and hell: the 'Great Mother' in Susa, with a dove as symbol, ruled supreme as queen of heaven, and a serpent as symbol, as the queen of hell.

Ishtar ruled the Babylonian world, Astrate the Semitic, Keybele the Greek and Isis the Egyptian world. In Indian mythology, one needs to think of Shakti cults and the tantrik mystery cults which at one time ruled the entire Eastern part of India from centres like Kanakhya.

Even in the world that was ruled by female deities, public or social authority was always with man. Woman's role was dubious and often ambivalent: sometimes they were queens, sometimes women were at the helm of a tribal government, sometimes they were magicians, sorceresses, priestesses—but only too often just slaves.

It is time for us to question for ourselves whether the religions of India have in any way been an enslaving, dehumanizing force of women in history. Have the interpretations of these religions coupled with the socio-cultural traditions at the various periods of history, been a contributing factor towards treating women as inferiors, non-persons, commodities that could be abused, sexually exploited sold? In the context of the above mentioned facts, let us examine the three major religions of India, *i.e.* Hinduism, Islam and Christianity.

HINDUISM

The concept of femaleness in Hindusim presents a duality. On the one hand the female is seen as divine, creative, nurturing and supportive and on the other, she is considered to be the epitome of all that is dangerous, carnal and evil and, therefore, in constant need of control and subordinatcon by the male. Hindu religious texts abound in opinions about women who is simultaneously seen as creative/good and destructive/evil. She is consequently both elevated and devalued,

In H nduism creation starts with godhead which is conceived of as a unity containing both male and female principles. Brahma, the Creator, is supposed to be half male and half female. At the moment of creation Brahma causes his body to separate into two distinct parts *purusha* (male) and *prakriti* (female) and it is this union of the male and female principle which leads to creation.

The Lord (*Prabhu*), dividing his own self into spirit (*atman*) and body (*deha*) becomes half male and half female (Manu, 1.32). Woman along with man is seen as a direct emanation from the divine body and is thus a part of his divine self. The female shares the original power of Lord Brahma, and therefore feminine power is divine power. The spiritual equality of man and woman is thus established. Another observation one could make is that the feminine principle is creative. When *prakriti* conjoins with *purusha* it results in the creation of the world. Here the female is seen as complementing the male to create. Thus, the female is seen as a divine and creative power.

Separated from the male, her power is seen as dangerous and malevolent. In Hindu mythology the feminine principle, not conjoined with the male and not under his control, is represented as Kali, the symbol of irresistible power and chaotic energy which may be dangerous. Watt (1969) explains:

"Kali is the embodiment of the Terrible Mother, the Spider Woman, the all devouring man of the abyss, image of everything of which the human soul seems ultimately to be afraid. On the other hand, she is eternal womanhood, cherishing mother of the world." (Watts, 1969: 84).

The belief that this power is a potentially destructive force when unrestrained, (that is, when not under male control), is reflected in the popular myth of goddess Kali performing her famous victory dance after killing a giant demon. In a bloody rampage she kills and destroys everything in her path without any control. When Siva, her husband, is sent to restrain her, he lies down at her feet. Kali, entranced by her killing, does not notice him and is about to step on him when she realises it is her husband and stops her rampage. Thus, when her husband regains control over her, the earth is saved. Thus Kali is depicted as the embodiment of destructive power when unrestrained, but when under the control of her husband, she is subdued. The benevolent goddesses in Hinduism are those who are married and who have transferred control of their sexuality to their husbands (Wadley, 1976). Thus the female deity under the control of the divine male transmutes into a benevolent being, and the male becomes the dominant member of the pair. In other words, the restraining social relationship of marriage subdues the dangerous forces of the female. In religious symbolism a married woman thus undergoes a basic transformation—from a dangerous species to a loving wife, the source of wealth and happiness. Thus the male acts as a restraining factor and becomes supreme by subordinating and subduing his female *shakti* in marriage. It is against this background of the essential nature of femaleness that the Hindu ideal of womanhood can be derived.

The Hindu idea that the female *shakti* has to be controlled by the male leads to the perverted idea that men have the right to subdue all women. Even men's sexual exploitation of women is justified on the grounds that the female spirit must be curbed wherever it is met, whoever the woman is. Carried to its logical conclusion reven rape can be justified by these arguments from scripture.

The basic rules for women's behaviour excerpted from different religious texts stress the need to control women because of the evils of the female character. Woman by nature is considered to be a deceitful and wily creature. She is deprecated in the following words:

"With women there can be no lasting friendship; hearts of hyenas are the hearts of women." (Rig Veda, 10.95.15)

In the Ramayana woman is described as unstable and restless:

"This has been the nature of the fair sex from the commencement of creation; that they gladden him that is well off, and forsake a person in adversity. And women imitate the instability of lighting, the sharpness of weapons, and the celerity of the eagle (*garuda*) and the wind." (Aranya Kanda, 3:13; Dutt, 11, 535).

Woman is seen as existing for the pleasure of man 'to gladden him'. She is the concubine or the Devadasi who exists for his fulfilme.it, physical or religious.

'The slave, the son and the wife (these three) are always dependent. They can have no wealth; for whatever they possess belongs to their master.' (Mahabharata, Sabha Parva, 2.17.2; Dutt, II, 9).

Woman's sexuality is seen as dangerous and, therefore, the religious texts lay down very strongly that a woman should always be protected by a man and never given independence.

The dependence of woman on man is total and absolute. Manu even allows man the liberty of beating his wife if she dare disobey him. Moreover, these religious texts frightened women into submissiveness by very vividly describing the hell-like existence she would have to lead in her future life, if she dared to disobey her father or husband in this life. Manu has said:

"By violating her duty towards her husband a wife is disgraced in this woild; (after death) she enters the womb of a jackal and is tormented by diseases, (the punishment for her sin)." (Manu, V, 165).

A woman in the scriptures is seen as a temptress, diverting man from his meditation. She is a hindrance to a man who would follow the path of holiness. She is the one who ensnares him with her wiles and therefore in Hindu society it is the woman who receives all the blame attached to prostitution while the man is allowed to go scot free.

The ideal of Sita, the heroine of the Epic, Ramayana, is placed before every Hindu girl. Sita's story emphasises the fidelity and chastity of the Hindu woman. She is worshipped as an ideal woman, uncomplaining, and a silent sufferer. The story of Ramayana revolves round the capture of Sita by the demon Ravana and the battle that follows between Rama and Ravana with Rama emerging victorious. Sita, forcefully separated from her husband, starves her body with the most severe kind of asceticism and remains pure, both in body and soul. Even when incessantly assailed by the demon, she is immovably faithful to her husband, Rama. Despite her fidelity and chastity, Rama publicly announces his suspicion of her character and refuses her as she had lived with a strange man. Rather than question the justification of her husband's conduct or waiver in her loyalty to him, she willingly subjects herself to a test of her purity of mind and soul. She jumps in to a pyre and comes out unscathed, establishing her purity and chastity. Sita is wholly the Indian ideal of a woman. She is called:

'O stainless one' (5.56, Dutt, II, 1056).
'Illustrious wife of Rama' (5.58, Dutt, II, 1˘68).

Rama's words to her reinforce the mores of the male-dominated society in which the lived, where a woman is the one punished for a crime committed against her. "Whatever I did was for the sake of avoiding scandal in every way and for the sake of clearing the name of the reputed dynasty. . . How can I accept you as such and sully my great family?" asks Rama. (Valmiki Ramayana, Yuddha Kand).

The Hindu concept of double standard of sexual morality can be seen where a woman, as idealised in Sita's case, is expected to remain a faithful, chaste wife at all times, while a man on the other hand should be worshipped as a God whatever his failings and shortcomings are.

"Though destitute of virtue, or seeking pleasure (elsewhere) or devoid of good qualities, (yet) a husband must be constantly worshipped as a God by a faithful wife."
(Manu, V. 154).

Another even more devastating feature of the Hindu scriptures is their emphasis on treating women as the property of men. "Whatever hypocritical politicians and (ignorant) Hindu jingoists might say, the sanction for the treatment of women as property is deeply embedded in our holiest traditions." ('Who's Afraid of Rape', *India Today* August 1-15, 1930).

Because woman is a form of property owned by man, rape, sati, bride-burning—all are justified. Women can be disposed of as the lord pleases. Even in Rig-Veda the concept of a woman's usefulness centres around her sexuality. The Brhadaranyaka Upanishad clearly permits and encourages rape. If a woman refuses to yield despite flattery and bribe, the man is advised that he should hit her with a stick or with his hand, and overcome her saying "with glory I take away your glory." Thus she becomes inglorious. (Brhadaranyaka Upanishad Brahmana IV, vii). "No stigma is attached to the rapist. Thus the great perceptor of the gods, Brhaspati, suffered no punishment for raping a married woman—the punishment fell on her child who was born blind." (*Rape, Society and State*, People's Union for Civil Liberties and Democratic Rights, Delhi).

Although Hinduism attributes the origin of man and woman from the godhead (Manu, 1.32), yet in actual practice, today centuries after scriptures were written, in the present, sociocultural setting, the oppressive caste system and traditions, our women and children are far from being considered as human beings, persons with dignity, worthy of respect.

ISLAM

The pre-Islamic social structure was tribal and is referred to as *jahilliyyah* (*i.e.* a period of ignorance) in Islamic literature. The Quranic revelations provided people with the knowledge of how to combat *jahilliayyah* practices. Tribal society has no written or revealed laws, only customs and usages; so had the pre-Islamic Arab society. The customs and usages, sanctified by age-old practices, were followed, irrespective of whether they were unjust or oppressive to certain sections of society. The only argument in their favour was that they found their forefathers following these practices. They argue with the prophets, 'How can we forsake what we found our forefathers upon?'

They said, 'Hast thou come unto us that we should serve Allah alone and forsake what our fathers worshipped. (The Quran 7:70, 11:62, 14:10, 16:35, etc).

In pre-Islamic society there were many abominable customs and usages in respect to women. During this period, there were no norms and laws as far as divorce, marriage, inheritance and property rights of women were concerned. One could marry women as one liked, could divorce them any time without any obligation as to maintenance.

In Quran ('The Koran—Penguin Classics—Founder Editor E.V. Rieu (1944-64)' p. 356. traditional No. Chapter 4 in Quran) it is clearly stated that the Lord created man and woman. The followers of Allah are exhorted to show great compassion, concern and consideration with regard to women's needs and rights, *e.g.* 'Men shall have a share in what their parents and kinsmen leave. Whether it be little or much, they are legally entitled to their share . . . Believers, it is unlawful for you to inherit the women of your deceased kinsmen against their will, or to bar them from re-marrying . . . treat them with kindness . . . If you wish to divorce a woman in order to wed another, do not take from her the dowry you have given her, even if it be a talent of gold . . . '.

Yet, thinkers and compilers of Shari'a were certainly influenced by their own milieu which was predominantly male-dominated. The Prophet was extremely kind to women, but the constraints of the male-dominated environment influenced his decisions also. 'It is related,' says Prof S.T. Lokhandwala, 'that on one occasion the Prophet said: "Beat not your wives". Then Umar came to the Prophet and said, "Our wives will get an upper hand over their husbands from hearing this". He also claimed that the Quraish (the tribe of the Prophet) always ruled their women and the Ansars (the people of Medinah) were always ruled by their women. So the Prophet agreed to keep the Arab social custom unchanged.' What was permitted in a certain social context and with great reluctance was taken by men as licence.

Muzammil Siddiqui, in her article, 'Impact of Islam on the Status of Women from the Socio-cultural point of view' states:

'The institution of marriage was, of course, not unknown but it did not confer on them any rights. The bride-money, *mehr*, was paid to the fathers or brothers. After their mariage, they could be sent to other men whom their husbands considered to be nobility, so that the husbands could boast of their offspring . . . They could be forced into prostitution with select persons and when a child was born, the man who resembled it was declared the father. A man was free to have any number of wives, concubines and slave women.'

Chapter four of Quran (related to women) further states that all women other than those specified in Quran, are lawful to men, provided they seek them with their wealth in modest conduct, not in fornication.

We found that the Holy Quran brought about a fundamental change in the women's needs and rights. It recognised and sympathised with their plight. They were recognised as human beings with rights. Infanticide was totally prohibited. Still, the Holy Quran does not confer equality on men and women. The Quran declared in unambiguous terms, 'and they (women) have rights similar to those (of men) over them in kindness, and men are a degree above them. Allah is Mighty, Wise.' (The Quran 2:228). It is said that, 'Men had authority over women because Allah has made one superior to the other, and because they spend their wealth to maintain them.'

The evidence of two women witnesses is equal in weight to the evidence of a single man. (*Religion and Society*. Religions and Women's Status. Vol. XXXII, No. 2, June 1985 pp. 20-42).

A Muslim woman has the right to inherit from her deceased father, husband and son. She has the right of payment of her unpaid *mehr* at the dissolution of her marriage, at the death of her husband or by divorce. Her share was, however, one half of what her male conterpart would get.

So we find in Islam, as in Hinduism, the origin of man and woman attributed to God, yet in actual life they are treated as inferior, subordinates, non-persons.

CHRISTIANITY

In the creation story, for both man and woman life originates with God. Neither man nor woman are autonomous creatures. Both owe their origin to divine mystery. 'And God created man to his own image, to the image of God He created him. Male and female He created them.' (The Holy Bible. Genesis I-27).

He did not make one sex superior to the other. It is this that gives human beings, persons, their significance and importance. They share with God freedom, dignity and responsibility.

Unfortunately one particular story—the second story of creation and the fall—has served to establish a wrong view that in the eyes of God and the world, man is destined to dominate woman and woman is condemned to subjugation and dependence (Genesis 2-3).

The coming of Christ was the beginning of new life and hope especially for women. Women were regarded as inferior beings and were categorized with children, calves and cattle. Women's place in society was as belonging to man—his property, which he could dispose of as he wished, to the extent of sacrificing her life to save his own; and her importance in the family was as a bearer of progeny.

In this historical context Jesus' attitude towards women was striking. He deals with women as persons, worthy to be talked to, listened to, worthy, being part of his band of followers, in need of salvation equally with men. He gave the Good News to all that God is our loving Father and we (men, women and children) are all His loving children. All belong to God's own family of Love.

Yet, in the New Testament, St Paul, the greatest of the Apostles of Christ, though accepting women as disciples, would not refrain from placing them in the secondary role. In Ephesians 5:22-24, he admonishes the women, 'wives, submit yourselves to your husbands, as unto the Lord. For the husband is the head of the wife, even as the Church is subject to Christ. So also let the wives be to their husbands in all things.'

Karl Barth was the courageous defender of human rights during the Nazi oppression of the Jews, yet he could not break loose from the traditional concept of the roles of women and men.

When we examine early Christian anthropology, we find a tendency to correlate femaleness with the lower part of human nature in a hierarchical scheme of mind over body, 'reason over passions.' Since this lower part of the self is seen as the source of sin and death—the femaleness also becomes linked with the sin-prone part of the self.

Augustine is the classical source of patriarchal anthropology. Although elements of it are present in the New Testament and in earlier patristic theologians, St Augustine expresses all aspects of it explicitly. He is in turn the source of this type of anthropology for the later Western Christian tradition, both Catholic and Protestant, who look to St Augustine as the fount of orthodoxy. Although St Augustine concedes woman's redeemability and hence her participation in the image of God, it is so overbalanced by her bodily representation of inferior, sin-prone self that he regards her as possessing the image of God only secondarily. The male alone possesses the image of God normatively.

Tertullian accused Eve of being the "devil's Gateway".

St Thomas Aquinas adopted the Aristotelian definition of woman as a misbegotten male. He reasons that even in the original created state, woman's defective nature meant that she was by nature servile and under subjugation. This created a problem for Aquinas. Why would woman be created at all, given that God should not have created anything defective in the original plan of things. Aquinas concludes that woman, although defective and misbegotten in her individual nature, nevertheless belongs to the overall perfection of nature because of her role in procreation.

Aquinas believed that males naturally excelled at the higher faculty of reason; females have less rational capacity and are less capable of moral self-control. According to him, good order requires that the naturally superior rule the naturally inferior. Aquinas believed in class hierarchy and slavery as necessary for social order.

The Dominican inquisitors Kraemer and Sprenger exempli- fied women as the personification of evil with occult powers like witches and consorts of devils.

Martin Luther says that in the original creation, Eve would have been equal with Adam. Therefore Eve was not like the woman of today. Her state was far better and more excellent. . . She is now within the fallen history, subjected to the male as her superior. This subjugation, Martin Luther states, is not a sin against her, but her punishment for her sin.

For Calvinists, even more than Luther, however, domina- tion and subjugation represent the original divinely created order of things.

Thus we find from the earliest times women are not conside- red as images of God, but rather of sex and evil. They are held as the eternal seducers—cause of all temptation and sin from the very first pages (Genesis 3).

In spite of Jesus Christ's proclamation that God is our loving Father, we (men, women and children), are children of God, persons, living temples of God—who will rise with Jesus Christ after death (Resurrection)—yet in human society women have been for centuries, and are still being treated as dependent, enslaved, sexually exploited at will, as inferiors, non-persons.

Conclusion

An analysis of a few selected passages from the Scriptures (Hinduism, Islam and Christianity) reveals that our origin, as male and female, is from God; that men, women and children are human beings, persons, in whom God dwells. We are the living Temples of God. Having seen in detail what it was and is, one can conclude, that this common thought that runs through all religions of India has been distorted by persons. It is evident from the details presented that the Patriarchal system has been safeguarded, while the condition of women and children has deteriorated.

Societal influences resulting from the enslaving aspects of religions, traditions, socio-cultural practices, economic and political roots, have contributed towards dehumanizing and degrading women and children. This is reflected in the following chapters on commodification, sexual exploitation and sale of women and children in India.

4

SCOPE AND METHODOLOGY

Sexual exploitation and sale of women and children is a phenomenon that is probably as old as mankind. It has not always been recognised to its fullest extent and in its widest implications. Scarcity and absence of up-to-date statistics on the subject does not mean that sexual exploitation of women and children does not occur in our country.

Exploitation of Children

Recently an increasing international interest has focused on the exploitation of children. Various governments, voluntary organisations, inter-governmental organisations and individuals combat the exploitation of children, to a greater degree than ever before. Probably more children are exploited today than ever before due to the simple fact that there have never been so many children in the world.

The history of mankind is like a nightmare if we look at it from the child's points of view, recognising the basic rights that we have begun to acknowledge for our children. But even today many children are exploited throughout the world—children who are pushed into hard labour, children who become part of adult conflicts, children who are abused for the benefit of adults and children whose sound development is impeded because the adult world in general is not ready and willing to allocate enough resources for the benefit of children.

A study conducted on raped, kidnapped and abducted children in a hospital reveal that of 100 cases of kidnapped children 93 per cent were girls. The age group of these children ranged from 3-16 years. Motives behind kidnapping were ascertained to be prostitution (3.4 per cent), selling (4.5 per cent), begging (4.5 per cent), employment and bootlegging (51.6 per cent) vengeance (3.5 per cent) sexual gratification (29.1 per cent) and for use as domestic servants (3.4 per cent). (Sumen Somen K. November-December 198ು).

One of the gravest forms of exploltation is the sexual exploitation and sale of children for prostitution. It has been very eloquently highlighted by Professor Ronhdika, who wrote the United Nations report on exploitation of child labour. The report states: "Child prostitution is, together with sale of children, the most distressing part of the story. There has always been a demand for children for sexual purposes because of their freshness and simplicity. Our age, which is permissive and at the same time surfeited and sexually vulgarized in the extreme, seeks all kinds of erotic refeshments. There is a great demand among our contemporaries for the sexuality of the child, through which they seek to renew their thoroughly jaded sexuality.

The experts argue over whether the actual rate of child abuse is rising or just the reporting of it. Either way, only a small fraction of all abuses are reported. No one really knows the actual situation.

In prostitution customers continue to demand younger and younger children to sexually serve them. What men seek, when they are buying sex as a commodity is various forms of perversions and sadistic activity. The physical and psychological effects of sexual exploitation are severe.

What is the extent of child prostitution in India?

In India, either through precocious marriages or use of small girls in prostitution, hospitals have revealed *haemorrhaging*, ruptured vaginas and uteruses, lacerated and mutilated bodies, peritonitis, venereal disease and even death resulting from sex relations between these children and much older men. Such a child cannot sustain pregnancy and child birth. Sometimes she labours up to six days and, unable to withstand the process, her body is torn apart and she dies.

The sad fact is that sexual exploitation and sale of women and children will continue until all those crimes are reported. It could be said that sexual exploitation and sale of women and children are the most under reported crimes in India.

Need for the Study

India is a society where sexual exploitation and sale of women and children is not regarded seriously. It is winked at, rationalised and allowed to continue through a complex of customs and mores that applaud male aggression and desire.

During the Women's Decade and the International Year of the Child several studies on exploitation of women and children were taken up. However, no in-depth study on sexual exploitation and sale of women and children was undertaken. This study aims at a more comprehensive and in-depth study on 'Sexual Exploitation and Sale of Women and Children in India'.

Scope and Methodology

The focus of this chapter is the scope and methodology of this research. For consistency in our understanding of certain terminologies used in this study, the following definitions are adopted.

Child means a boy or a girl who has not attained the age of eighteen years.

Minor means a boy or a girl who has not attained the age of twenty-one years.

Man means a male who has attained twenty-one years.

Woman means a female who has attained twenty-one years.

Adult means a man or a woman who has attained twenty-one years.

The Concise Oxford Dictionary—New Seventh Edition (1983) defines Exploitation and Sale as follows:

Exploitation: to utilize person or persons for one's own ends.

Sale: exchange of a commodity for money.

Sexual Exploitation means to utilize person or persons sexually for one's own ends.

Sale means 1) to exchange sex as a commodity for money.

2) to exchange person or persons as commodities for sexual exploitation for money.

Objectives of This Study

1. To explore whether sexual exploitation and sale of women and children exists in India.

2. To study the demographic background of the victims of sexual exploitation and sale.

3. To detect within the specified period as many forms or types of sexual exploitation as possible that women and children are subjected to.

4. To ascertain the mode of entry, recruitment, the process of victimization adopted prior to initiation into the flesh-trade, the price tags for the women and children in India and the age of initial sexual exploitation.

5. To discover the trafficking pattern of women and children in the flesh trade; to locate the flesh-triangles; the demand, transit and supply centres in our country.

6. To identify persons (structures) directly responsible for the initiation, maintenance and promotion of sexual exploitation and sale.

7. To conscientize the public at large of the magnitude of this problem and awaken/elicit/stress the need for a joint, concerted/sustained effort as citizens of India to eradicate sexual exploitation and sale in India.

8. To suggest measures that would create a society where

   (a) our women and children will be acknowledged for their worth as human beings, persons with human dignity and rights, (not commodities to be sexually exploited and sold), to be truthfully loved and respected.

   (b) sexual exploitation and sale will be eradicated.

Universe and Sample

Keeping in mind the objectives of the research, an interview schedule was formulated and sent to 35 experts in India for their perusal and critical evaluation. The experts included heads of departments of social work, sociology, psychology, psychiatry, dermatology; heads of government and voluntary agencies engaged in services to the victims of sexual exploitation and sale, heads of religious institutions, counsellors, research committees, etc. A pilot study was conducted towards the end of 1983 in Bangalore City. As there was evidence of inter-state trafficking in women and children, this research originally confined to Karnataka State, was thrown open to the whole country.

For this exploratory, time-bound study a purposive sampling technique was used, keeping in mind the need to include as many respondents as possible and the various contemporary forms of prostitution/sexual exploitation. Identification of the victims of sexual exploitation and sale is extremely difficult. Besides, the secrecy that shrouds this problem and the lack of adequate material on this topic in India, made it more difficult to prepare a framework of reference to select sample units on a probability basis.

Various techniques were adopted to identify and interview cases. In a majority of cases clusters were identified at random as sample blocks, especially in 'red light' areas, government and voluntary organisations where victims are placed, National Highways, Devadasi and Basavi belts; and remote areas of 'scheduled caste and scheduled tribe' communities.

To obtain samples of victims of massage parlours, virility tests, blue films, film extras, call-girls, cabaret artists, etc., suburban and highly developed metropolitan cities were visited.

For the sample of 'street walkers', etc., the researcher had to sit at the bus stands, street corners, railway stations at odd hours.

To get the sample of women and children under bondage and strict surveillance from some of the *Silent Zones* of our country, the researcher had to seek the assistance of the police from Karnataka and Maharashtra. For treading these areas meant not only assault in the person but high risk of being murdered. In these states during her field work, both men and women police were provided by the government as protection.

During data collection, Bombay (Maharashtra State) proved to be the highest risk area. In Guntakal (Andhra Pradesh), while waiting for the train the researcher was offered a purse by flesh-traders (which she refused to accept). In Bellary (Kurnataka State), during her night travel she was stopped on the road by a policeman on suspicion. The researcher was also exposed to a new form of molestation, eve-teasing at Madras City (Tamil Nadu).

A research study of this nature involves great risks—this was expected prior to venturing into this study. But what surprised the researcher was that in spite of her advanced age she was subjected to eve-teasing, offered a purse, and was on the verge of being arrested on suspicion! One wonders at this rate whether our society is safe enough for the movement of our young women and children.

The sample both in terms of primary and secondary data, selected for the study are presented in Table I. Further state-wise distribution of 'red-light' areas of primary data collection are given in Table 2.

As the problem taken up for the study was extremely sensitive and deals with delicate personal issues, an interview schedule was developed.

TABLE 1

Distribution of data: States and Union Territories

Sl. No.	States/Union Territories	Primary Data	%	Secondary Data	%	Total	%
1.	Andhra Pradesh	273	43	1	.2	274	24.9
2.	Assam	—	—	1	.2	1	.1
3.	Bihar	25	3.9	9	2.	34	3.1
4.	Gujarat	1	—	2	.4	2	.2
5,	Jammu and Karhmir	—	—	19	4.1	19	1.7
6.	Karnataka	149	23.5	126	27.	275	25
7.	Kerala	—	—	1	.2	1	.1
8.	Madhya Pradesh	—	—	18	4	18	16
9.	Maharashtra	42	6.6	98	21.1	140	12.8
10.	Orissa	16	2.5	3	.7	19	1.7
11.	Rajasthan	—	—	16	3.4	16	1.5
12.	Tamil Nadu	52	8.2	23	5.	75	6.8

(Contd.)

13.	Uttar Pradesh	43	6.8	34	7.3	77	.7
14.	West Bengal	24	3.8	5	1	29	2.6
	Union Territories						
1.	Chandigarh	–	—	1	.2	1	.1
2.	Delhi	11	1.7	1108	23.2	119	10.8
	Total	635		465		1100	
	%	58		42		100	

TABLE 2

Red Light Areas of Data Collection

Sl. No.	State/Union Territories	Cities/Towns/Rural Areas where red light areas of data collection are situated
1.	Andhra Pradesh	Hyderabad/Secunderabad, Adoni, Vijayawada, Cuddapah
2.	Bihar	Muzaffarpur
3.	Karnataka	Banglore, Bellary, Raichur Dist. Belgaum Dist., Bijapur Dist.
4.	Maharastra	Greater Bombay, Pune, Nasik Dist.
5.	Orissa	Koraput, Jeypore Nagarampur
6.	Tamil Nadu	Madras, Madurai, South Arcot Dist. Madurai-Madras Highway
7.	Uttar Pradesh	Allahabad, Kanpur, Varanasi
8.	West Bengal	Calcutta/Howrah, Bankura West Midnapore
	Union Territories	
1.	Delhi	G. B. Road, Delhi

While the main method used is descriptive this has been further substantiated with case studies and statistical interpretations.

Limitations of the Study

The main limitations of this national level study has been due to lack of time which came in the way of obtaining substantial data and evidence. *e.g.*, witnessing the system followed by the 'Dark World'—'Irunda Ullagum' of Tamil Nadu.

The second limitation can be attributed to the non-usability of a definite structure in certain situations as indicated below:

1. Being a research at the national level, the researcher had to seek the assistance of several field workers and interpreters with the knowledge of local languages, layout of the 'red light' areas, etc. The interview schedule sent by the researcher was not followed by some of the field workers.

2. The presence of customers at the time of interview especially those in a drunken state, interrupted free communication and loss of vital information.

3. In *Silent Zones*, *e.g.*, of Bangara Camp in Manvi, Raichur District and some areas of Bombay's 'red light' area, communication with the victims was not possibile. If they had responded truthfully it might have ended up in physical and mental torture after the researcher left the place. In these situations just observations or non-verbal communication was utilised.

4. Some of the respondents were highly infected with STD, some suffered from mental illness, a few carried sticks and long knives to protect themselves from molesters. Talking to these persons meant a high risk of being misunderstood or attacked.

5. In metropolitan cities interviewing film extras, girls involved in blue films, etc., was found difficult. These persons were paid by the film industry, or private individuals. They had very little time to spare. They have to adjust to the timings of the team's working hours.

As some of the above mentioned items indicate, information received from these persons was incomplete.

6. With regard to secondary data, especially police publications in the daily newspapers, very few details are given. While ascertaining the ages of women and

children, the researcher had to omit several cases as she was unable to interpret terms such as 'young girls', 'young women' etc. As per SIT Act, the terms clearly state 'girls' are between 18 to 21 years and 'women' those who have attained 21 years.

5

TYPES OF SEXUAL EXPLOITATION

The previous chapters set out the objectives of the study and began to meet the first two of them. It showed that cases of exploitation of women are recorded in India and are on the increase. It pointed out, however, that there is under-reporting of those crimes and great unevenness between reports from different states (p. 10, 11). This study has therefore taken a fresh look in fourteen states and two union territories to find out the true picture (Table 1 and 2). In this chapter the third objective of the study is taken up, "To detect within the specified period as many forms or types of sexual exploitation as possible that women and children are subjected to." After a general intro-duction, the study sample of persons is analysed to see the different kinds of exploitation. Finally the most common types of exploitation, with social or religious sanction, are examined in detail.

Markets of sex deal in a variety of 'flesh' to suit the tastes and pockets of various categories of customers. If a man has money and/or high position/status he can buy without difficulty the girl/s of his choice. In Tamil Nadu, for example, there are the 'Reception Centres' where, on payment, the customer is directed to the desired 'commodities.' Places such as milk booths are used as reception centres.

There are special 'driving clases' organised by flesh-traders for those interested. Fees for these coaching classes are collected by the organisers of the flesh-trade. Under the guise of teaching driving, persons are taken up and down safely to the hotels and places of prostitution.

'Virility tests' are recommended for the 'patients' in five star hotels. Referrals are made by the professional doctors on payment of· large sums. A beautiful girl is made available to these 'patients'. The sample in the present study shows that a girl from Andhra Pradesh, after a stay in a hotel in Bangalore, Karnataka, was in Tamil Nadu at the time of data collection. The girls are moved from place to place.

In order to defeat the law, the flesh traders adopt various contemporary forms of sexual exploitation and sale of women and children. Trafficking our women and children into prostitution has become a highly profitable market in our present society. For a better understanding of the situation in India, we shall begin with the analysis of the data.

TABLE 3

Types of Sexual Exploitation

Types of Sexual Exploitation		State	Number of Respondents
1		2	3
1. *Prostitution with Social Sanction*			
Dancing girls	(11)	Andhra	10
		Delhi	1
Singing and dancing girls	(4)	Bihar	1
		U.P.	3
Singing/dancing concubinage	(15)	Bihar	8
		U.P.	7

(Contd.)

1		2	3
2. *Prostitution wtth Social and Religious Sanction*			
Basavis	(200)	Andhra	200
Devadasis	(48)	Andhra	15
		Karnataka	33
Kalavanthulu	(2)	Karnataka	2
3. *Prostitution with legal sanction*			
Marriage with Arabs	(1)	Karnataka	1
4. *Prostitution with no legal sanction*			
Brothel	(324)	Andhra	2
		Bihar	17
		J. & K.	9
		Karnataka	48
		M.P.	1
		Maharashtra	113
		Orissa	16
		Rajasthan	15
		Tamil Nadu	25
		U.P.	22
		West Bengal	18
		Delhi	38
Roadside Prostitution	(26)	Andhra	22
		Karnataka	2
		Tamil Nadu	2
Prostitution in Lodges	(35)	Karnataka	35
Prostitution in Hotels	(18)	Karnataka	2
		Maharashtra	14
		West Bengal	2

(Contd.)

1		2	3
Blue film Prostitution	(1)	Karnataka	1
Highway Prostitution	(7)	Tamil Nadu	7
Street Walkers	(12)	Karnataka	9
		Tamil Nadu	2
		Delhi	1
Prostitution in lodges and brothels	(22)	Tamil Nadu	22
'Floating' girls	(1)	West Bengal	1
'Maidan' girls	(1)	West Bengal	1
'Camp' Prostitution	(9)	Karnataka	9
Prostitution at roadside and railway station	(8)	Andhra	6
		West Bengal	2
Prostitution at home	(7)	Andhra	6
		West Bengal	1
Sale of liquor cum prostitution	(1)	West Bengal	1
Prostitution at man's residence	(2)	Andhra	1
		Delhi	1
Cabaret Artists Prostitution	(38)	Karnataka	27
		Delhi	11
Concubinage	(4)	Karnataka	4
Acting in films	(4)	Tamil Nadu	4
Massage Parlour	(1)	Maharashtra	1
Music cult sexual exploitation	(1)	Karnataka	1
'Marriage', Mistress	(25)	Gujarat	1
		J. & K.	8
		Maharashtra	6
		U.P.	10

(Contd.)

1		2	3
Marriage/Mass Marriage and Desertion	(6)	Karnataka	4
		Delhi	2
Virility tests in Posh Hotels	(1)	Tamil Nadu	1
Call girls	(71)	Karnataka	34
		Maharashtra	1
		Tamil Nadu	1
		Delhi	35
Changing from person to person concubinage	(3)	Karnataka	1
Nights with different sets of young men	(1)	West Bengal	1
Free Sex	(2)	Delhi	2
Call girls/concubinage	(9)	Karnataka	8
		Delhi	2
		Tamil Nadu	1
Child Prostitution	(2)	Assam	1
		Kerala	1
5. *Trafficking*			
Trafficking in children	(9)	Uttar Pradesh	9
Trafficking in women	(1)	Madhya Pradesh	1
Child lifting	(4)	Karnataka	4
Sale of children with mothers	(1)	J. & K.	1
Offer of sale of infant	(1)	Karnataka	1
6. *Rape, etc.*			
Gang rape of minor	(1)	Andhra	1
Sexual exploitation of minor	(2)	Karnataka	1
		West Bengal	1
Sexual exploitation of domestic workers	(2)	Karnataka	2

(Contd.)

1		2	3
Sexual exploitation of construction workers	(9)	Andhra	6
		Bihar	3
Gang rape	(10)	Gujarat	1
		Bihar	3
		Karnataka	1
		Maharashtra	2
		Delhi	1
		Chandigarh	1
		Rajasthan	1
Gang rape and stabbed to death	(1)	Orissa	1
Rape	(19)	Andhra	1
		Karnataka	3
		Madhya Pradesh	8
		Maharashtra	2
		Delhi	5
7. *Arrested*			
For not obliging the police	(1)	Karnataka	1
Arrested on suspicion	(2)	Karnataka	2
8. *Engaged in Homosexual activities*	(1)	Karnataka	1
9. *Others*			
Forms of Prostitution not specified	(85)	Andhra	1
		Gujarat	1
		J. & K.	1
		Karnataka	36
		Madhya Pradesh	8
		Orissa	2

(Contd.)

1		2	3
		Tamil Nadu	2
		West Bengal	16
		Delhi	18
Attempted rape	(1)	Maharashtra	1
N.A.	31	Total	1100

The following are the various forms or types of sexual exploitation and sale to which the victims in the sample were subjected.

An analysis of the data of the 1100 persons who comprise the sample reveal that 983 persons (89.3%) were definitely victims of sexual exploitation. Of these 324 persons (29.5%) were engaged in brothel prostitution and 250 persons (22.7%) were involved in prostitution with socio-religious sanction. 197 persons (17.9%) were subjected to various forms of sexual exploitation as mentioned above. The rest of the people in the sample, 117 persons (10.7%), were brokers, madams, persons rescued before sale or sexual exploitation and customers and those whose form of prostitution was not specified.

Since brothel prostitution and prostitution with socio-religious sanction were numerically the two major kinds of sexual exploitation recorded in the sample a description of these two types is appropriate.

1. Brothel Prostitution

The main distinguishing feature of this type of prostitution is that the victims of sexual exploitation are traditionally found in areas called the 'red-light' districts, areas recognised by the public and the police for this purpose.

It is generally presumed that these persons enter prostitution voluntarily, having an idea of what is expected of them.

According to the *Illustrated Weekly of India*, November 26, 1972, there were 2000 brothels spread all over the city of Delhi.

"Kidnapped as children, abducted as teenagers or lured to the cities in young adulthood in hope of employment, the lives of thousands of women and children are destined to be circumscribed by the four walls of a brothel. Accommodation is shared with fellow inmates which is not only insufficient but also unhygienic. Whether the customers are ill or well, ugly or handsome, young or old, sober or drunk, suffer from mental illness or are under the influence of drugs, the women and children are bound to accept them".

As Table 14 reveals, these persons brought here mostly by violent means are cut off from everyone. They are generally permitted very little freedom of movement and remain under strict surveillance of the brothel keepers or hired men. New environment, new name, new language, coupled with illiteracy, low image of themselves as a result of being born in communities designated as low castes, lack of funds and powerlessness, often make them submit to the existing situations in the brothels. They succumb to the treatment meted out to them, leading to submission.

Table 3 indicates that of the total 324 persons engaged in brothel prostitution at the national level, 113 persons (34 per cent) belong to Bombay brothels. An analysis of the sample under migration and trafficking in women and children reveals that the victims of sexual exploitation and sale in Bombay brothels belong not only to Northern and Southern India, but also to Nepal.

Amrita Shah, (*Imprint* September 1984) states that the influx of Nepali girls to Bombay brothels began 7 years ago. These women in the course of time became *gharwalis* ('Madams' of the Brothels). They bought or brought girls from Nepal for the flesh trade in Bombay. A single Nepali girl can fetch up to Rs. 50,000 for the flesh traders. Uneducated and totally unexposed to the world they are duped easily. Parents far off in Nepal make enquiries but are often too poor to follow-up negotiations of their daughter's whereabouts. In some cases, even if they accept money from their daughters (earned through sale of sex) they are not prepared to accept the girl at home.

The character traits of these Nepali girls, of submission and honesty, also make them popular with customers for they not only accede easily to their demands but also return even small change owed to the customers. These factors along with the Indian fascination for fair skin, saw the demand for their services. It is estimated that there are 20,000 Nepali girls in the Bombay, 'red-light' area. Her rate can go as high as Rs. 3000 per night if the customer happens to be a rich Arab.

Women and children from India, especially from the South, find this invasion of Nepali girls a threat to their livelihood. When business declines these girls are in a pitiable condition. They are ill-treated, pushed out to the streets to solicit customers, made to stand for hours. If sufficient cash is not brought in for their own expenses, to pay back their 'debt' (amount paid by the gharwali or broker at the time of purchasing the girls), etc., the girls are beaten up and starved.

In 'red light' areas, the researcher passed through *Silent Zones*. The women and girls are strictly forbidden to talk to people. Their relationship with customers ought to be just a 'business' relationship. These girls were suffering from venereal diseases.

There are days, festival seasons, when business is high. During this period far too many customers are thrust on these girls. Later these girls suffer from abortions, etc.

On the whole motherhood is denied to these women and girls. Those with children experience problems such as lack of privacy, finance for maintenance of children, involvement of sons in the flesh-trade and the sexual exploitation of girls at a tender age. The Secretary Indian Health Organisation had estimated as early as 1982, that there were 70,000 women and children in Bombay's 'red-light' area (*The Darby*, Bombay February 13, 1982).

Suresh Kohli in his article 'Bombay by Night' (*The Illustrated Weekly of India*, October 31, 1982) states: "The city of Bombay comes alive when most other places in the country have yielded to the demands of the sunset. Madras turns grey,

Delhi brown, Calcutta black. But Bombay is always blue, the neon and mercury lights assume a different hue. Just as the sea changes colour, the city transforms itself.

"A three-storied building in Santa Cruz was raided after policemen from Andhra Pradesh traced a girl in a flat on the second floor. Two hundred and ten girls in different costumes and age-groups were found in twelve two-bedroom flats. With the rate for a girl ranging from Rs. 500-700, the entire co-operative's turnover amounts to as much as Rs. 1.2 lakhs per night. After deducting percentages for the 'Keeper,' his assistants, the girls, etc., the remaining (about 50 per cent) went to the house owners who had invested Rs. 20 lakhs in the building. From this house they could earn about Rs. 18 lakhs per month. Similar enterprises are in Colaba, Bandra, Juhu, Versova. Two men, 'Kings,' earn Rs. 10-15 lakhs a month— "They have enough," writes Suresh Kohli, "to buy MPs and MLAs".

Although there are some commonalities with regard to brothel prostitution in India one can easily observe certain trends, changes, traits which distinguish one brothel from the other.

Traditionally customers are received in brothels but in Bombay it is not uncommon to see women and children taken to hotels and lodges for customers. In G.B. Road brothels in Delhi we find the singing and dancing girls. The call-girls visit G.B. Road brothels on a part-time basis. The Chaturbhuj Sthan of Bihar, originally meant for singing and dancing girls around the temple of the ancient deity, has given way to thronging women and girls of varied social, economic, lingual and emotional backgrounds. The women and children in the brothels of the drought stricken areas of Karnataka are different from the women who function as 'surrogate wives of Shonagachi, who serve the well-to-do men of Calcutta. Whatever the commonalities or variations in brothel prostitution, it can be concluded that the presence of 'red-light' areas in India or as a matter of fact in any country in the world, is a sign of subjugation of women and children, commodification and sale of persons. It reflects the low status of women and children, indicates male dominance and speaks of the under development and decadence of a country.

One thing is certain, whatever the variations of life-style, economic situations, etc., these women and children have two options, they are either thrown out on the street when useless or they die of a sexually transmitted desease that goes untreated.

As Captain Colabawala in his book *Sex Slaves of India* (1981) rightly says, "Prostitutes wear out fast, and when they are no more useful they are discarded and thrown out into the street. The unfortunate old prostitutes stand hopefully against the wall plastered with hired cinema posters, or pound the pavement or just stand in rains and stare or die as rabid dogs do—unwanted and unwept."

2. Prostitution with Socio-Religious Sanction

The second highest form of sexual exploitation and sale comes from the group under the heading: "Prostitution with Socio-Religious Sanction."

Table 3 shows that 200 Basavis, 15 Devadasis and 2 Kalavanthulus of Andhra Pradesh and 33 Devadasis of Karnataka in all 250 persons (nearly 25 per cent of the total sample) comprise this group.

A detailed description of the 200 Basavis and the various aspects of their exploitation will be dealt with under Chapter 7. In this chapter the Devadasi system and the Kalavanthulus (Shangu Chakra) will be taken up. The discrimination among the dedicated persons, the male and the female, the Jogis and the Jogithis in the Devadasi System; the caste/class syndrome of this system, the extent of sexual exploitation and sale of children, minors and the transit centres of flesh trade will be highlighted.

THE DEVADASI SYSTEM

From the semantic point of view Devadasi means "Maid of God." The Devadasi system is broad-based wherein a man or woman who is ushered into this system through the rituals stipulated for the purpose gets installed into the system, in the presence of gods and goddesses as the case may be. According to the tenets of this systems, from the moment a man or woman enters in to this system, he or she should devote her entire life to the service of gods or goddesses, in whose name he or she enters into the system. The belief is strong among those who dedicate themselves that they get purged of their incurable sins and thus attain salvation.

Different forms of this system prevail in India today, with a mythological source, a religious sanction and a traditional mode. For example the legend of Yellamma-Renuka, adopted with many variations from the Aryans, relates the story of Sage Jamadagni and his pious wife, Renuka.

Renuka, it is said, used to fetch water for her husband's ritual in a pitcher made of sand, using a snake as a head rest to carry the pitcher. One day while she had gone to collect water, she noticed Gandharvas, frolicking in the water. Even as the thought that she could have married a handsome Gandharva and lived in luxury if she had wanted crossed her mind, the sand pitcher crumbled in her hand. She lost the divine power she had gained through her chastity and purity.

During what had transpired in her mind, her sage husband became enraged and ordered her sons to behead her. The two elder sons refused but the youngest, 12 year old Parashurama, agreed to do his bidding.

Pleased, his father offered Parashurama three boons. The boy implored his father to restore his mother to life. The sage then asked him to get the head of a 'Matangi' (a low caste woman) and fix it to the trunk of his mother, where upon she came back to life. Thus Renuka, brought back to life, is worshipped as a goddess more so by the members of the Matangi clan and then girls are offered to her to be wedded for use by her son, Parashurama.

Dedication: The dedication of a girl is similar to that of marriage. The girl to be dedicated in most cases would not have attained puberty. Once she is dedicated she is barred from marrying. Once she attains puberty she is in the market. The patron has the privilege of spending the first night with the girl. She spends anywhere between Rs. 100-800. This celebration is called 'Hennu Madurvudu' or 'Manni Maduvidu' (in some areas 'Gejje Poorje)-nuptials or deflowering.

Nipani in Belgaum district is one of the main points in transit in the girl traffic pipeline to Bombay. Nipani is the main tobacco trading centre on either side of the Karnataka-Maharashtra border . . . . the town has about 800 prostitutes of whom 200 are Devadasis.

Athani is one of the major transit centres. It is a prosperous trading town and forms one side of the Teradal-Mangooli-Athani triangle, famous for prostitution. Athani has a 5000 strong Harijan community organised into about 500 families . . . 98% of these families practice prostitution. There is migration from nearby villages of families of Harijan community.

In the *Bijapur Dist* the Devadasi belt touches Maharashtra. All the taluks have devadasi system. Tikota, which has a Hanuman temple, is one of the major centres of dedication in the district.

Haunsoor district is famous for its Devadasi and ordinary prostitutes who are recruited to the numerous drama groups of north Karnataka. The town has been the traditional supplier of girls to these drama groups and companies from Gadag and Haveri, etc. (The Devadasi Problem in *Banhi*, 1981/82, an occasional journal of the Joint Women's Programme.)

1. *Discrimination*: As per this system males and females could get dedicated. Males are called Jogis. They are permitted to marry. The children of these Jogis can become Jogis and Jogithis.

With regard to Jogithis, these women cannot marry. If a paramour keeps her as a mistress for a definite or indefinite period, his off-spring has no right to take the name of the father—the child can only bear the mother's name.

As a result of discrimination between Jogis and Jogithis, the children of Jogithis are discriminated against at various levels *e.g.* at school they are considered as 'fatherless' children-born out of wedlock.

2. *Class/Caste Syndrome*: Mathungi was a scheduled tribe. As the Table 9 indicates most of the Devadasis belong to scheduled tribes and other scheduled castes. These are normally from the lower economic groups. The class/caste system reinforced by the myth coupled with socio-religious sanction has become a complex problem of caste as also class exploitation by vested interests.

3. *Sexual Exploitation of children, minors*: Free for all sexual pleasure sanctioned by religion and easy money earned through prostitution provide an incentive to the parents and guardians of the child to dedicate children, minors—even before birth at times.

Besides, sexually exploited by rural rich, minors are sent or taken to urban areas, where they are sexually exploited by urban rich. Unofficial estimates reveal that the 'Yellamma spinsterpool' supplies five thousand damsels for the flesh-trade in Bombay and Pune, annually.

THE KALAVANTHULA SYSTEM

Among the Hindus of Cuddapah District, it was an ancient custom to bring the diety around the city in a decorated chariot for public worship. At one of these festivals, a beautiful young girl is selected to offer incense to the diety defore the chariot leaves the temple.

At this ritual, soon after the young girl offers the incense to the diety installed in the chariot, the celebrant—the guru who officiates at the function—puts a conch in the fire and then brands the girl's two upper arms with 'Shangu-chakra' *i.e.*

conch wheel. These marks (branded portion) while forbidding her from marrying, sanction her sale of sex (Prostitution).

The researcher observed that of all her respondents in this study in South India, this group—Kalavanthulu—were the most highly literate and economically well off.

6

PROFILE OF THE SEXUALLY EXPLOITED

The study wanted to find out the background of the victims of sexual exploitation and sale. This chapter examines the data of the sample in order to give details of the age at the present time and at the time of initial exploitation, the sex, religion and caste, education, marital status and migration pattern of the victims.

Age

'The National Policy for Children' of the Government of India's Ministry of Social Welfare, New Delhi quotes (pg 17) the UN declaration on the Rights of the Child (1959):

"Principle 9 states: The child shall be protected against all forms of neglect, cruelty and exploitation. He shall not be the subject of traffic in any form".

The sample reveals, however, that there is sexual exploitation of children in India and that those who are exploited or sold are in fact usually children (*i.e.*, under 18 years old) at the time of their initial exploitation.

An analysis of the data indicates that 384 persons (35%) of the sample were children below 18 years; 208 persons (19%)

TABLE 4

**Age of the Victims of Sexual Exploitation at the Time of
Data Collection**

Age-Range	Age at the time of date Collection	
	Frequency	Percentage
Below 18 years	384	35%
18 — 21 years	208	19%
28 — 30 years	231	21%
30 years & above	155	14%
Not applicable	122	11%
Total	1100	100%

were girls between the age of 18-21 years; 592 persons (54%) of the sample were minors. This gives us evidence of child prostitution and sexual exploitation of minors in India at the time of data collection. The table further reveals that 231 persons (21%) were between the age of 21-30 years and the remaining 155 persons (14%) were above 30 years, *i.e.*, adults. An analysis of the age of initial sexual exploitation gives shocking information.

The Table 5 shows that more than half those who are sexually exploited are children (53%) and more than three quarters are minors (76.5%).

At this point some details and observations related to 'age' in the flesh trade will be dealt with. The system followed by the Khattawallahs or money lenders of Falkland Road, 'red light' area of Bombay, is like this: young girls below the age of seven, either kidnapped or obtained by force, threat or payment by middlemen are sold to the brothel keepers and kept with these Khattawallahs.

TABLE 5

Age of Initial Sexual Exploitation of the Victims Engaged In Prostitution

Age at the time of initial sexual exploitation	Victims of sexual Number	exploitation Percentage
Below 18 years	585	53.2
18 — 21 years	259	23.3
21 — 30 years	48	4.4
30 years and above	1	.1
NA/Not available	210	19.0
Total	1100	100

The Khattawallahs and the brothel-keepers are bound by a mutually beneficial commercial agreement. The Khattawallahs pay for the food, clothing and general unkeep of the girl till such time as they are old enough to join the brothel. Files are maintained by them in which the amount spent is jotted down regularly every week. After a period of around six to seven years when the girl has crossed the age of puberty she is collected by the brothel keeper and absorbed in the business.

Part of the earnings of the girls are used to pay off the debt accumulated over the years. 'It usually takes the girl around five years to clear the debts. By then she is. . . . beyond rehabilitation. 'Buying and selling of Indian women'—Magazine '*FOR YOU*'—June, Fortnight, 1978, Vol. III. No. 12 Pg. 11).

Most of the victims initiated into prostitution with social, religious and legal sanctions are mere children, *e.g.* The Basavi, the Devadasis, those offered in marriage to Arabs, etc. Many of the victims trafficked from Northern and Southern regions of India and from Nepal are minors. Even some of the so called 'married' women who are forced by their husbands to

Comparison of Tables 4 and 5

AGE OF INITIAL SEXUAL EXPLOITATION OF VICTIMS OF FLESH TRADE		AGEGROUPS	AGE OF VICTIMS OF FLESH TRADE AT THE TIME OF DATA COLLECTION	
RESPONDENT %				RESPONDENT %
585	53.2	18 Years and below		584 35
256	23.3	21 Yrs.-18 Yrs.		208 19
48	4.4	30 Yrs.-21 Yrs.		321 21
1	0.1	30 Yrs. and above		155 14
210	19.0	DATE NOT AVAILABLE		122 11

trade, were sexually exploited as children. Child marriage still exists in India. Some young girls were even raped/sold/forced into prostitution by their fathers.

This study reveals that the youngest brothel-keeper was a boy of 14 years; the youngest victim of sexual exploitation was a one-year-old baby and the youngest child for sale was an infant in the mother's womb bartered for Rs. 3,000.

Women and children subjected to the flesh trade do look much older than their actual age for various reasons, *e.g.*, due to lack of sleep, malnutrition, burdened with too many customers, abortions, pregnancies, effects of venereal diseases, pollution, bad ventilation, tuberculosis, etc. Due to this fact at the time of arrest a girl below 18 years is taken to be 18 years and above and confined in institutions meant for 18 years and above. (These young girls get acquainted with brothel keepers, child-lifters, etc. In one institution I was told by a person in authority that the girls in her institution sleep like husband and wives. Those with disease exchange clothes with those who are well. Those who are brought for protection are taken advantage of by fleshtraders. Mothers with infants and toddlers are restricted to certain areas.)

Sex

In India the position of a female child from birth is vulnerable as the sex ratio statistics show.

TABLE 6

Sex Ratio in India 1901-1981

The sex ratio, number of females to every 1000 males, decreased steadily from 1901-1971. In 1981 there was a slight increase as seen below.

Year	Females	Year	Females
1901	972	1951	946
1911	964	1961	941
1921	955	1971	930
1931	950	1981	935
1941	945		

Many factors contribute to the decline. The unwelcome female child, ill-fed, and neglected, showed a higher mortality rate than males. Mother's health affected adversely due to excessive child bearing meant death during sickness. Ever nuturing others, malnutritioned women succumb to illness. Infanticide added to the death toll.

S.H. Venkataramani in her Article 'Female Infanticide: Born to Die,' *India Today* June 15, 1986) states roughly about 6,000 female infants were poisoned within a decade in Usilampatti Taluk, in Tamil Nadu, South India.

According to demographers, the number of women in the Chambal area has been registering a downward trend. Among some communities like Gujras, Thazurs and Brahmins, the situation is grim. Marriage becomes difficult for a Brahmin girl out of caste. In olden days, some Takurs and Gujras used to kill their daughters at the time of birth. This practice was prevalent in Rajasthan till recently. There are some villages which have not witnessed a girl's *barat* (wedding party) for about 200 years. (Patronage of politicians, *Indian Express*: 1-5-84).

In our patriarchal society a woman or girl is perceived by the SIT Act as a criminal. The women and children are considered as the main source of venereal disease. *e.g.* in Tamil Nadu venereal disease is called *Penpal Noi i.e.*, disease pertaining to the female gender. Society speaks of 'fallen women' but never 'fallen men'. Our double standard in morality permits a man to swear fidelity to his decent 'wife' on the one hand and visit the 'woman of vice' on the other. A man going to a woman is considered 'natural' while a woman going to a man is considered 'unnatural'. On one hand society justifies men going to women in the flesh trade by saying there are more men compared to women (the ratio between men and women in India), on the other hand they do not welcome a female child. Female children are uncared for, unfed and even killed— thus bringing down the ratio of females in our country.

In 1931 the population was 683,310,051 of whom 330,500,000 were women. The life expectancy for the males and females during 1961-71 was 47.1 years and 45.6 years respectively, unlike developed countries where women live longer than men,

(Ashok Mitra, ICSSR. *The Status of Women's Literacy and Employment*, New Delhi, Allied Publishers; *Women in India*—A Statistical Profile, Government of India, Department of Social Welfare, New Delhi, Ministry of Education and Social Welfare).

TABLE 7

The Population of India in 1971

Total persons	54,31,59,652
Males	28,40,49,276
Females	26,41,10,376
Females Rural	21,37,25,732
Females Urban	5,03,34,644

Patriarchal class society has really posed a major threat to the survival of women in India. As far back as 197 , Professor Ashok Garg had given us a warning signal to the fact that continuous decline in the sex ratio of female to male would pose a grave problem for Indian society. He had declared women in India as a 'declining sex.'

The women in the flesh trade suffer not only in a gender biased society for being a woman, but are forced to degradation through commodification and sale for sexual exploitation, for man's utility. She is confined to sexual and reproductory roles and denied the right to the blossoming of her personality, the total development as a person. This is evident from the sample of this study. Although the researcher went about looking for both male and female victims of the flesh-trade, during her data collection, 98 per cent of the data *i.e.*, 1079 persons happened to be females. Only 2 per cent were males (21 persons). This shows the high degree of sexual exploitation of females in our country, when compared to males.

Girls born in families such as singing and dancing girls are doomed to a life of sexual exploitation. Taroon Coomar

Bhaduri in 'A shameful Tradition' (*Statesmen*, 15th January 1984) states, "Obscurantist Hindus have always, down the ages, frowned upon the birth of a daughter because of a future dowry demand. But not the Banchchras. For them, the birth of a daughter in the family is a blessing, in as much as she is a potential economic commodity up for sale . . . . There is revelry in the village and liquor and meat flow freely on the night a girl is 'initiated.' The first customer foots the bill. There are 200 Banchchra girls at the moment being prepared and groomed to take up this profession in the name of tradition and religious custom. The eldest daughter of a family must become a prostitute and support the rest of the family . . . every night, interspersed with the sobs and sighs of many a teenaged girl, the world's oldest profession goes on."

The vulnerable position of a female child at its very birth can be seen from the above examples. The process of socialization of girls, while it prepares them to play the roles society expects of them, also makes them vulnerable. They are so thoroughly conditioned to accept an inferior position in society that even the so-called present-day "emancipated" women seem to suffer from this complex.

A New Delhi based psychologist, Sudhir Kaker, says: "Even some of my middle class or upper class clients who may appear to be emancipated and have reason to lead a fairly contented life, suffer from this I-am-worthless-because-I-am-a-woman trauma beneath their veneer of emancipation. They continue to live their traditional role of believing themselves to be inferior, inadequate and worthless beings. Hindu Society remains a dominantly partriarchal society. (ndia Today 1 August, 1980).

Dehumanisation is an essential aspect of this condition. Women from childhood undergo a slow process of destruction of or devaluation of self-worth. They have interiorised the inferior self-image thrust upon them by the menfolk so deeply that anyone who tries to speak up against it would seem to go against the aspirations of women.

Another result of this conditioning is that a woman's value as stated in earlier chapters, seems to be judged, not so much in terms of her worth as a person with rights and dignity, as in terms of her utility to man. She is considered by man, either father, brother or husband, as a socio-economic gift to his household, as a commodity to be disposed of, by the father to the husband, implying in most cases that she is not welcome in the parents' house, if she should be exploited. Her parents may reluctantly take her back but her foothold in their house remains precarious. She is there on sufferance, not by right as are sons. Part of the justification used by many families for refusing to provide support to their daughter is that they have done all they could. Their responsibility is over. In India, for every baby boy abandoned by the parents, five baby girls are deserted by them. (The *Liberation of Women* CRI Patna Unit, Fr. Joseph Velamkunnel S.J. Article: 'The Christian Response to the Exploitation of Women', page 18.

Religion and Caste

In the Indian society which consists of many communities professing diverse religious faiths, religious tradition becomes of paramount importance in understanding the relative status of women and men.

TABLE 8

Religion of Respondents

Religion	Frequency	Percentage
Hindus	428	38.9%
Muslims	41	3.7%
Christians	40	3.6%*
Buddhists	1	.1%
Sikhs	1	.1%
Religion not known	589	53.5%
TOTAL	1100	100.0%

*Most of the respondents were from South India. This accounts for the high percentage of Christians.

Caste as defined by eminent sociologists is a hereditary, endogamous, usually localized group having traditional associations with an occupation and a particular position in the local hierarchy of castes. Relations between castes are governed, among other things, by the concepts of pollution and purity and generally maximum commonality occurs within the caste (Sriniwas 1978).

Though caste is practised to a greater extent by the Hindus, some of its features have affected other religions too. Further, Hindus being over 80 per cent in India, the dominant practices are of the Hindus—Brahmanical and patriarchal values prescribed by the 'law giver' Manu. In one of his codes he mentions, "Be a girl or a boy, a young woman or a woman advanced in years, nothing must be done even in her own dwelling place, according to her pleasure." Thus as per Hindu religion and caste values, a woman should be self effacing, self-denying, self-sacrificing and submissive.

TABLE 9

Caste of Respondents

Sl. No.	Caste	Frequency	Percentage
1.	Brahmins	5	0.5%
2.	Lingayats, Agriculturists Artisans	57	5.2%
3.	S.C. and S.T.	415	37.7%
4.	N.A.	623	56.6%
		1100	100%

An analysis of the data on caste of respondents indicates, Table 9, that 415 persons (37.7 per cent) of the sample belong to scheduled caste and scheduled tribes. Only 62 persons (5.7 per cent) belonged to other 'Upper Castes.' There is no information with regard to caste from 623 persons (56.6 per cent). This reveals most of the victims whose caste is known, come from the scheduled caste and scheduled tribes. A few who came from 'upper class' enjoyed better facilities, etc., provided by the politicians, and rich patrons. Whether the victim of sexual exploitation comes from lower caste or upper caste she is looked down on by society.

Simone de Beauvoir in his book *The Second Sex* pp. 568-569, states—"Sewers are necessary to guarantee the wholeness of palaces, according to the Fathers of the Church and it has often been remarked that the necessity exists of sacrificing one part of the female sex in order to save the other and prevent worse troubles, so, a caste of 'shameless women' allows the honest women to be treated with the most chivalrous respect. The prostitute is a scapegoat, a man vents his turpitude upon her, and he rejects her. Whether she is put legally under police supervision or works illegally in secret, she is in any case treated as a pariah."

It is sad to see that in spite of a comprehensive piece of legislation in India—The Civil Rights Protection Act of 1976—which covers not only social but also economic oppression, there still exists a high degree of sexual exploitation and sale of women and children belonging to the so called Scheduled Caste and Scheduled Tribes.

Table 10 indicates that 130 persons (11.8 per cent) have attended school. This 11.8 per cent includes persons other than victims of sexual exploitation *e g.*, male customers, brokers, bothel-keeper, etc. 576 persons (52.4 per cent) have had no schooling in any form and can be considered as illiterates. With regard to education no information was available from 394 persons (35.8 per cent). In our vast country female illiteracy amounts to about 80 per cent. Illiteracy of the majority of the victims has contributed towards their vulnerability in the flesh trade racket. Flesh traders prefer an illiterate, as a it is easier for them to extract conformity to their wishes. It enhances the communication gap, both verbal and written, in a strange land which proves ideal for procurers and madams who trade on them. The victims of sexual exploitation due to illiteracy are at a loss, unable to communicate their plight either to those around them or to their family.

TABLE 10

Education of Respondents

Sl. No.	Education	Frequency	Percentage
1.	Persons with education	130	11.8
2.	Persons with no education	576	52.4
3.	Information not available	394	35.8
	TOTAL	1100	100

Inspite of the government's compulsory education schemes and non-formal education programmes, this section of women and girls continue to remain illiterate. The flesh traders deprive them of the services extended to all sections of the society by the government. There is an urgent need to reach out to these persons, very specially to the children in 'red-light' areas with various educational schemes.

Table 11 on Marital Status indicates that 728 persons of the sample (66 per cent) of the victims of sexual exploitation are unmarried women. Only 16 per cent, 172 persons were married. This shows the demand for the unmarried girls in the flesh trade. Men for various reasons *e.g.,* pleasure, fear of contacting venereal disease, etc., go in for virgins, unmarried girls. This can be seen from the examples cited above. The flesh traders who are aware of the market demand, try to procure children, unmarried girls and make a flourishing trade out of the whole flesh racket.

TABLE 11

Marital Status of Respondents

Marital Status	Number of Respondents	Percentage
Unmar ied	728	66%
Married	172	16%
Information not available	200	18%
Total	1100	100%

With regard to married women who comprise 172 persons (16 per cent) in the sample, there were fake marriages, girls purchased, married and sold, married, raped and put in a brothel; married at 'Mass Marriage Functions' shortly after that raped, their wives carried away their little belongings, etc., and disappeared—Table 18. Persons responsible for entry into prostitution—depicts that 47 husbands have forced their wives into prostitution.

In Secunderabad, married women in construction work are sexually exploited. Married women in Vijayawada, Andhra Pradesh and South Arcot District in Tamil Nadu move to highways and byways for prostitution. These women are either forced or encouraged to enter this life by their husbands and parents. In many cases these men take to alcoholism. In Karnataka, some of the women after their marriage come to know that their husbands are pimps and procurers in the flesh trade. Due to lack of skills and with very little or no education they are unable to live economically independent lives. Quite a number stay with their husbands and submit to forced prostitution for the sake of their children. A married woman in our society may visit her parents, stay temporarily but soon the parents and society tells her that her rightful place is in her husband's home. Rarely parents and society question these women's husbands for the treatment meted out to these women. They are convinced that once married, the girl is the property (commodity) of her husband. He is free to do whatever he likes with her. The girl has to consider him as her lord and god. She is expected to submit to him till death. Married women in this study are exploited at home by their husbands and parents and in-laws and outside their homes by men, as in the case of construction workers, etc., while they go to earn their daily bread.

The marriage patterns of these women show that with socio-religious and legal support minors are married to men much older than them—some are fit to be their grand-fathers in age. We find that the very institution of marriage itself is used by these unscrupulous men to subjugate and force their wives to prostitute. Those who rebel against this exploitation are tortured, strangled, stabbed to death. While some attempt suicide, others, the voiceless get resigned—it is our 'fate', 'karma' 'kismet', 'God's will', they say.

Gulf-marriages in Hyderabad city, Andhra Pradesh, South India, have touched a new high in recent months, with as many as 500 *niqahs* solemnised with the tourist Arabs.

According to Mr. Mohd. Ishaque Gulshani, a social worker and trade unionist, at least 99 per cent of the Arabs marrying Indian girls leave the country once their tourist visa expires, promising to send the necessary documents and money to enable the wife to join them, but are never heard of thereafter. According to the police, the fugitive husbands pay between Rs. 500 and Rs. 3000 to the 'wives' they desert. The girls are left with little after meeting the Qazis and the brokers' claim. (*Deccan Herald*: 17 August 1982 from the Correspondent).

A 13 year old girl was married to an 85 year old Arab. Parents of this economically poor girl received Rs. 2000 in cash and 28 grams of gold. The Arab tourist after his arrival in Calicut, Kerala, South India, contracted a broker for a bride. The girl belongs to the village Murath. The girl's mother lives with her second husband (*Thina Thanthi*, 14. 2. 85 Madras).

Migration

In the country as a whole intra-state migration and migration from outside the country are minimal. At the 1971 census 30.42 per cent of India's population were migrants numbering 166.6 million. 67.8 per cent were women, very nearly the same as that of 1961. Women seem to predominate in short distance rural—rural migration. The major reason attributed to the rural—rural migration of women in India is marriage. Table 12 shows the pattern of migration for 1971 (census of India 1971, paper No. 2 of 1979 Migration in India, Ministry of Home Affairs, New Delhi, 1979).

TABLE 12

Patterns of Migration (1971)

Female (All India)

Rural to Rural	77.50 per cent
Rural to Urban	10.48 ,,
Urban to Rural	5.03 ,,
Urban to Urban	6.67 ,,
Unspecified	.32 ,,
Total	100.00

An analysis of the migratory pattern of the victims of sexual exploitation and sale reveals, as depicted in Table 13, that out of 1100 persons in the sample 326 persons (29.6 per cent) were inter—state migrants:

TABLE 13

Migratory Pattern of Respondents

No change/change within the vicinity	308	28%
Inter-state migrants	326	29.64%
Intra-state migrants	128	11.64%
Rural-urban or urban-urban	149	13.54%
No information available	189	17.18%
Total	1100	100.0 %

The next highest number, 308 persons (28 per cent of the sample) have had no change or change within the vicinity itself. The Basavis, Devadasis, married women, etc., come under this group. The Basavis and Devadasis have had the support of society and religion. Quite a number of women remained with their family members and carried on prostitution in a clandestine manner at the insistence of their husbands, guardians, etc. Sexual exploitation of married construction workers and details of trafficking in women and children are dealt with in Chapter 8. Of all the migrant women, the sexually exploited section of migrants face more problems. This seems to be the plight in East Asia. The following report gives a similar situation in Thailand.

"Since the adoption of the first National Economic Development Plan of 1961, it has seen considerable economic, social and political changes. Many studies on migration clearly indicate that during the programme of national development and industrial expansion there has been a greater incidence of intra-rural and rural-urban migration. Bangkok is the most important reservoir of rural migrants. Female migrants have particularly increased in numbers during the decade 1960-1970 according to the Thailand National Statistical Office, 1963 and 1973. The same statistics show that at present the number of female migrants in Bangkok exceeds those of male migrants.

As for the problems that women migrants face. . .the group that has the highest number of hardships is that of prostitutes." (Suthinee Santaputra, problem of Improverished Women Migrants in Bangkok Metropolis, *Women in Development*, pp. 64 and 69).

7

RECRUITMENT AND PRICES

This chapter deals with the fourth objective of the study which is to ascertain the mode of entry into prostitution (recruitment), the process of victimization prior to initiation into the flesh-trade and the prices paid for women and children in India. It is generally assumed that most of the girls involved in the flesh trade are either lured or enter voluntarily. This study reveals that most have entered by forceful, violent means.

In the sample of 1100 persons (Table 14) it was found that 735 persons (67 per cent) have been forced into the flesh trade in 33 shocking ways. Only 124 persons (11 per cent) were lured. Details concerning the 241 other persons were not known or irrelevant (*i.e.*, they were the clients, madams. etc.).

An analysis of the 1100 persons of the present study has been given in Table 14, under 8 broad categories. A more detailed description of the manner of recruitment to prostitution and other forms of sexual exploitation noted in the sample is given in Table 15 below.

The flesh traders have developed patterns of victimization to dominate and coerce women and children into the flesh trade. Whether passive or violent forms of entry—whether lured, conditioned or forced—they are not aimed at the welfare of the individuals but geared towards sexual attacks on their bodies and also on their psyche. They form part and parcel of

Trafficking in Women and Children in India

TABLE 14

Mode of Entry into Prostitution

Sl. No.	Mode of Entry	Frequency	Percentage
	Violent Forms		
1.	Abducted/kidnapped/auctioned/sold and resold	124	11.3
2.	Deceived and sold	103	9.4
3.	Sold and resold repeatedly	100	9.2
4.	Raped/gang raped and sold	20	1.8
5.	Fake marriage/raped/deserted/forced	164	14.9
6.	Conditioned by religious custom (Basavi/Devadasi etc.).	224	20.4
	Total	735	67%
	Non Violent Forms		
7.	Lured	124	11%
8.	Not available	241	22%
	Total	1100	100%

the process of victimization, consciously designed to violate their sense of themselves, their female, human dignity. The combination of culturally designed moral debasement and physical battering are the methods adopted whereby women and children undergo a slow or rapid metamorphosis from 'respectable persons with dignity and freedom' to 'sellers of sex and slavery.'

TABLE 15

Methods of Recruitment to Prostitution

Methods	Freq-uency	Methods	Frequency
1. Abducted, kidnapped and sold	33	2. Abducted for sale	6
3. Auctioned	5	4. Gang raped, sold and resold	1
5. Fake marriage and sold	8	6. Marriage, sold and resold	1
7. Sold, purchased, married and resold	1	8. Concubinage for the highest bidder	8
9. Tribals sold	1	10. Child-lifting for sale	11
11. Kidnapped for sale, prostitution	49	12. Abducted, kidnapped, sold and resold	8
13. Deceived and sold	31	14. Deceived, sold and resold	3
15. Deceived, forced into prostitution, sold and resold	1	16. Repeatedly deceived and sold	2
17. Deceived, lured, sold	23	18. Lured for sale of unborn child	1
19. Deceived	36	20. Sold	64
21. Child sold with mother	1	22. Sold, resold	12
23. Repeatedly sold and resold	2	24. Sold, raped and resold	16
25. Raped, purchased, sold and resold	3	26. Raped,	12
27. Gang raped	3	28. Abducted, kidnapped, gang raped	2

(Contd.)

TABLE 15 (*Contd.*)

29. Deceived, raped	3	30. Married, raped and put in brothel	1
31. Mass marriage and desertion	4	32. Forced into prostitution	159
33. Conditioned/forced into prostitution through tradition or religion	224	34. Lured	12[4]
35. N.A.	241		
Total			1100

The vulnerable sections of our society (*viz.*, persons belonging to scheduled castes and scheduled tribes, children and minors, illiterate and the unmarried) are dehumanized, subjected to inter-state trafficking, etc. If conditioning or torture does not subjugate them, other forms of violent sexual assaults such as rape, gang rape, etc., are adopted.

Those who rebel against their exploiters are starved, whipped, burnt with cigarette or beedi butts, forced to drink intoxicating drinks, drugs or herbal concoctions, cut on the face, branded or locked up. In some cases those who have not bent to the will of their masters have committed suicide (*e.g.*, the case of the girl who jumped from the hotel window in Bombay was widely reported in the press).

The researcher's interview with the women and girls revealed that some were tricked into fake marriage. An illiterate woman was taken to court and made to execute an affidavit (which she could not read) leveling charges of cruelty, drunkenness or immorality against her husband. She then declared she had therefore severed marital ties with the husband as she had lived away from him for more than two years. This was followed by a new marriage. The new husband declared that he would keep the woman happy and make the offspring his legal heir. All the papers were executed on stamped paper and duly attested by a notary. The previous husband had no opportunity to challenge

TABLE 16

Methods of Subjugating Women and Children

1. Starved	2. Locked-up in a dark-room
3. Beaten up	4. Slippered
5. Gaged	6. Cut on the face with knives
7. Whipped	8. Branded
9. Burnt with cigarette and beedi butts	10. Raped/gang raped at the point of a knife, sharp weapons
11. Led to places desired by wielding of knives or pointing guns	12. Bound with strings and cords along with the use of knives to demand submission
13. Forced to drink intoxicating drinks, drugs, and herbal preparations	14. Blackmailed
15. Driven to commit suicide for not obliging sexually persons other than husbands	16. Strangled/stabbed/killed for not trading their bodies
17. Sexual exploitation of expectant mothers/bartering for the unborn.	

the allegations and lost his wife *in absentia*. The new 'marriage' was a means to procure the woman for prostitution.

Shocking as it may seem the researcher found that in many cases of 'sale of girls' it was the girls' own close relatives who struck the bargain, and sold their children for gains.

In Tamil Nadu poor Harijan girls fall prey to the flesh traders who pose as benefactors at the bus stops and railway stations. Usually the girls are looking for jobs as their alchoholic fathers or husbands do not provide for them. The girls come under the influence of agents in the flesh trade, who are mostly owners of liquor shops. Brokers approach the agents for the girls. The girls are categorised age wise 14-18 years, 18-22 years, 22-25 years, 25-30 years. The rate per girl is Rs. 2000, though some can fetch as little as Rs. 400-500.

Of the brokers that function on the Madurai—Madras Highway, 60 per cent are males and 40 per cent are females. These female brokers get the support of powerful men. Each broker has 5-10 girls and an area coverage of 4 km. The brokers have a common understanding; if a girl in her/his group gives trouble, or tries to run away, she is at once sold to another broker. At times if the broker suspects that the girls are getting friendly either among themselves or with the lorry drivers (their customers) they dispose of the whole group: they are sold off to other brokers. Food and clothing are provided by the brokers. At 10 p.m. they are on the road (National Highway). They call this the 'dark world' of prostitution.' 'Irrunda Ullagum.' In the dark the customers are unable to see the faces of the girls. I am told that of the Rs. 5 per customer, Rs. 3 is the broker's share, Re 1 is 'Puddie' 'Mamool' for police, and Re 1 for the girl. If the girl does not bring in Rs. 20-50 per night she is starved, slippered, branded, kicked, etc. Recently a girl while soliciting on the road desperately in order to earn at least Rs. 20, the minimum expectation of the broker, was killed in an accident. No one took notice of it. These girls are sold and resold several times. By the time they reach the age of 30 years they are infected either with STD, T.B. or mental illness. Many die, a few who are of strong constitution turn out to be brokers themselves.

The researcher during data collection visited one of the relaxing centres on the National Highway belt in Tamil Nadu. This favourite spot of the customers is situated in a beautiful place by the roadside, with a pool and thick vegetation that provides water and privacy for the flesh traders. The researcher had two married men and a married woman along with her. Although at their arrival at the spot the place was deserted within a few moments a couple of youths turned up to see them. They soon realised they had not come for girls and so left. They were eager to study the area as it was getting dark. They could see the condoms used and some unused strewn all around this pool. In their illiteracy and ignorance these young girls are taken advantage of by the flesh traders.

Of those introduced to prostitution through religious means, mention has already been made of the Devadasis and Kalavanthulu in Chapter Five. The researcher also came across the Basavi who live in Adoni, Andhra Pradesh, through the study carried out by the Joint Women's Programme, (*The Basavi Cult* JWP 1985). These women are recruited to prostitution by dedication as children to the Goddess Yellamma and they can never marry. The term 'Basava' means a bull which roams the village at will and points to the foot-loose position these women hold in society. They can be used by a patron for a long time for a fixed sum. They are always insecure and neglected by society. Their children have no legitimacy and without any husband it is difficult for them to get official recognition. (*e.g.*, when applying for house plot). They earn a precarious livelihood and many work in the ginning factories in Adoni. As G.G. 'Kakasaheb' Karkanis says, "The upper caste Hindus have skilfully used religion to establish an order of prostitutes who are licenced to serve them and made to feel they are fulfilling a religious duty into the bargain. They have very subtly destroyed the self respect of the lower castes to the point 'where dedicating a girl to prostitution seems in no way different from sending a son of the family to a village school'.*

In the flesh trade, the victim seldom gets the cash directly in her hand. Often her parents and guardians, brothel owners or the flesh-traders who trade on her accept the cash directly from the customers. Where a fixed rate is known by all, the cash is received by the victims, but a paultry sum is her share. In cases where inter-state gangs are concerned the bargaining is often done between the parties in the absence of the victim. In the case of auctioning the girl is aware of the whole process.

---

*G.G. 'Kakas heb' Karkanis (a Gandhian Social worker who dedicated his life to bringing about consciousness and education among the Scheduled Castes) in his book *Devadasi: A Burning Problem of Karnataka*.

The analysis of the data gives the following rates for the women and children of India as it emerged from the study.

TABLE 17

'Price Tag' for women and girls sold by flesh traders

Sl. No.	State	Market	'Commodity'	'Price Tag' —in rupees
1	2	3	4	5
1.	Andhra Pradesh	Proddatur Market	Badvel girl	5,000
2.	Assam	Darrang Mela	15 year old girl	9,000
3.	Bihar	Muffarpur	Bride Price, later sold	2,000
			Kidnapped, raped girl	2,000
			Kidnapped, raped girl	1,000
4.	Jammu and Kashmir	Gond Arahim village	A girl	500
			Another girl	1,300
			Another girl	1,600
			4 West Bengal girls (1)	2,500
			originally from (2)	5,000
			Bangladesh (3)	5,000
			(4)	20,000
			Two girls bought for 9000 were resold for 1200 giving profit of Rs. 3,000.	9,000 / 12,000
			Charge for showing a girl.	100

1	2	3	4	5
			Selling price demanded Rs. 12,000, settled for	10,000
5.	Karnataka	Bangalore	New born babe	3000
		Bombay	Women and children from Gokak, Mulbagal/	2000
			KGF and Bebbal	3000
		Athani	A very good looking Devadasi girl	10,000
6.	Madhya Pradesh	'Flesh Triangle' of Agra-Dholpur-Morena	Girl	5,000
			Same girl resold	8,000
			14 year old girl	4,000
		Morena (MP)	Beautiful girls in MP	4500
			other girls in MP	2200
7.	Maharashtra	Bombay V.T.	Teenager (lowest price)	400
			Same girl resold	500
		Bombay 'red light' area	Girl from Tamil Nadu	2500
			Others from Tamil Nadu	3000
			Girls from Andhra Pradesh	3000
			Girls from Karnataka	1000
			Others from Karnataka	1800
			Beautiful girls from Karnataka	5000
			Nepal girls	4000
			Special Nepal girls	50,000
		Bombay for (Foreign market)	A girl from Kerala	60,000
		Haji Malang, Rock cave Bazar near Kalyan (Auction sale)	A Muslim graduate girl	70,000

(Contd.)

1	2	3	4	5
		Pune 'red light' area	Girls from Tamil Nadu	1000
			Girls from Andhra Pradesh	1000
8.	Rajasthan	Guluwela village in Sriganganagar Dist.	A girl	4000
9.	Tamil Nadu	Arialpur, Tamil Nadu	A girl	500
		Pondi	A girl (same girl resold)	1,500
		Bombay market	A girl (same girl resold)	3000
		Madurai—Madras	A girl	1000
		National Highway	A girl	2000
		Belt i.e., Salem,	Same girl after 'use'	500
		Madurai, Viruda-chalam, South Arcot Dist.	Lowest rate for 'used' girl	400
10.	West Bengal	Sikandarpur village	A girl	1500
		Hooghly, Calcutta	Planned resale of same girl in metropolitan market	5000
11.	Delhi	Delhi	4 Adivasi girls from Nasik, Maharashtra	46,000
12.	Uttar Pradesh	Kanpur,	A girl	1000
		Benares	A girl	1500
			Another girl	2000
		Kaval Exporters i.e; Kanpur, Agra, Varanasi, Allahabad, Lucknow.	Ten thousand children sold at between one and two thousand each	1000 2000
		Allahabad	A girl	800
			Another girl	2000
			Another girl	4000
		Through a Maharastrlan pimp	A girl from Allahabad	3500

The rate per person depends mainly on the complexion, physic, and age of the girl. A virgin may fetch more than a non-virgin in spite of her better looks. In the Bombay Market Nepalis receive higher rates than girls from South India. A Nepali girl can fetch Rs. 50,000. *e.g.*, as already mentioned Rs. 70,000 was paid by an industrialist in Bombay for a Muslim graduate. This was at an auction. A Kerala girl who was duped by flesh traders and is back in India was sold to a foreign flesh market for Rs. 60,000. The Jammu and Kashmir rate goes up to Rs. 20,000 per person. The Delhi market rate shows Rs. 11,500 per Advasi girl from Nasik.

The study reveals that Bombay (Gateway of India) and Delhi (Capital of India) are the highest demand centres in the country. These are centres of tourism as well. Illiterates, minors, the unmarried, the economically poor, girls from scheduled castes and tribes are kidnapped, abducted, sold, resold, in order to cater to the demands of well-to-do men from India and abroad. Bombay market has the lowest rate, Rs. 400 as well as the highest. This shows that the flesh traders here cater to all sections of society and that the price of the girl depends on where she is sold.

Whether the amount paid for our women and children is significant or insignificant, smaller or larger, it is a *sale*. Whether cash is paid or not paid, the subjugation, objectification, commodification, non-personalisation of our women and girls for male utility and *sexual* exploitation is a sure sign of dehumanisation of our women and degradation of our society.

8

PATTERNS OF TRAFFICKING

The fifth objective of the study is to discover the trafficking patterns of women and girls in the flesh trade, to locate the 'flesh triangles', the demand, transit and supply centres in this county.

The study of secondary data *i.e.*, reports in newspapers and magazines, supports the findings from the sample in this study that the flesh trade in India is carried on at various levels—from international to local level. The *Times of India* 24.3.84 reports that inter-state trafficking in children has Kanpur as headquarters.

I. Karim in *India Today* 31.8.83 states that there is subcontinental trafficking in women organised by a gang operating across the borders of Burma, Pakistan and Bangladesh.

There is evidence from Britain that there is an international racket in selling 'wives' of Asian origin to Indians to beat the immigration laws in Britain. Fathers advertise their daughters and offer them to the highest bidder in India. Sums of $ 1000 are involved (*Deccan Herald* 28.11.82).

The analysis of the data reveals trafficking in women and children both at the state, (macro-level,) going right down to the local village, (micro-level). Trafficking in 12 states and 2 union territories has been recorded in the study.

1. ANDHRA PRADESH

Among the sample are the Basavi. The Basavi system is practised predominantly in the Harijan families of Adoni. There are eight scheduled caste bastis called Gher. There are two hundred Basavis in this area. 120 of them work in the ginning factories earning Rs. 200 per month. Others work as wood and grass cutters and casual labourers.

In the sample there are 15 Devadasis. They live in Ashoknagar. The researcher found this area very close to the bus terminus. This has been one of the general findings of the study *i.e.*, near bus stands, railway stations and market places there are always crowds and very near it 'red-light' areas are situated. The traffic and trafficking in women and children seem to go hand in hand. As the customers mostly come to their houses, there is very little movement.

Persons from Palamarru in Mahaboob District Vikrabad, Amul Basti, Maduray and neighbouring villages come to Secunderabad for construction work. These women are dependent on the men folk for their employment. Being in the unorganised sector, they have to yield to the men for their daily work. Sexual exploitation of women has become a daily affair among construction workers of this area.

Women and girls from Azttha Singnagar, Prakashanagar, Ganavaramu and Vijayawada town go to Guntur, Chilukalurpetta, Chirala bus stand, and lorry check posts, etc. for prostitution. Nearly half the locality go in for prostitution. These women and girls are either forced or encouraged by their husbands and parents to carry on this work. There is alcoholism among menfolk. Women are forced to earn through prostitution.

There are some dancing girls from Vijayawada included in the study. These girls move around with the organisers within the state. These dancing girls face sexual exploitation.

Allagadi, Mydukar, Roddathin are known for sale of girls for sexual exploitation. Some of these girls have been raped. In order to evade the wrath and ostracism of the family and society these girls of the lower economic group run away from their home. Flesh traders are always there to take them to brothels to sell them to other flesh traders. The 'Kalavanthulu' community, although dedication to gods has ceased, continue prostitution in their own houses, in Cuddapah District.

Persons from Warrangal, Parsigudda, Tarnaka, Tirmulgher move to Chilubeleguda Lal Bazar, Ramakrishnapuran, Secunderabad railway station for prostitution. There is inter-state trafficking between Madhya Pradesh and Hyderabad and Secunderabad; also between Andhra Pradesh and Maharashtra, Bihar, Tamil Nadu and Karnataka. In Vizayanagaram sale takes place on occasions such as the 'car' festival when girls are sold to Waltair in Andhra Pradesh and Jeyore in Orissa.

2. ASSAM

As the data reveals Darrang has bout 450 women trapped for prostitution. There is child prostitution. A 15-year old girl was sold by her maternal uncle for Rs. 9000. There is evidence of sale and sexual exploitation of tribals.

There is *Inter-State* trafficking between Bhutan and Darrang; Manipur and Assam.

3. BIHAR

Local residents of Harijan colonies in Muzaffarpur have been gang raped by the dacoits. There is some movement in this area: (*i.e.*, parents who work in agricultural areas or make their living through begging or send their children to red-light areas of Muzafferpur). Their is *Inter-State* trafficking in Bihar. Persons from Bettiah and Gaya are also seen in this place. Patna to Muzaffarpur, Gaya to Darbange are other trafficking intra-state movements seen in the sample. The *Inter-State* trafficking consists of Dholpur, Rajasthan to the 'red-light' area of Bihar, Muzaffarpur; Andhra Pradesh to Muzaffarpur. Outgoing *Inter-State* trafficking seems to be from Munger, Bihar to Baktikpur, Bangladesh and from Sanghbhum to Calcutta, West Bengal.

4. JAMMU AND KASHMIR

A Kashmir flesh trade scandal, in which about 500 girls from Bengal are reported to have been sold to various 'centres' in the valley, has been handed over to the state crime branch.

The girls, whose age group is said to be between 13 and 30 years, have been reportedly brought to Kashmir on the pretext of giving them "decent" employment or labour, but on reaching Kashmir, they are sold either to these centres or directly to the clients, normally rich old men in the districts of Badgam, Mupwara and areas outside Srinagar.

Several Bengali and Kashmiri commission agents have been selling the "brides" for anything between Rs. 5000 and Rs. 20,000 depending upon the beauty and youthfulness of the hapless girls. . . . These girls are kept in secluded areas outside Srinagar and tortured and locked up till they agree to do what they are told by the agents. (*Indian Express*, 4th June, 1984).

Data shows that nine victims were from poor Muslim families of Bangladesh settled in West Bengal and nine victims along with a child were from Virbum and Mushidabad settled in West Bengal. These persons were sold to Kashmiris; a year 9 old was married to a 40 year old man and a 15 year old to a 60 year old man. These girls were shown sharp weapons, beaten up and abducted. Some others were lured by the sweet talk about going for a holiday by the flesh traders.

5. KARNATAKA

Karnataka has sale, 'marriage' brothel, local, intra-state and inter-state trafficking of women and children. An analysis of the data collected in Karnataka reveals that the victims of sexual exploitation at the *local level* (in Bangalore city) come from Lingarajpuram, Sevanagar, Devajeevanhalli, Tannery Road, Kodahalli, Hal Road, Brigade Road, Ashoknagar, M.G. Road, Cubbon Park, Adugodi, Wilson Garden, Kalasapalaya, City Market, Chickpet and Balepet. Mostly Devadasis of the sample come from Mawi, Neermann, Indiranagar of Raichur

District, from Nipani, Gannagara and Shankaralathi, Athani in Belgaum.

A few samples have been included from Bangara camp, Manvi and Bellary Town as well as Bangalore City.

The next category of persons who are victims of sexual exploitation have some movement from their living area. If they leave their residence at dawn they can return by nightfall or if they leave at dusk they can return home the next morning. These persons are usually considered as working persons, either on day on night shifts. These persons come from the city itself, suburban and rural areas viz, persons from Rajajinagar, Dasarhalli, Lingarajpuram, Kanakapura, and Krishnarajpuram. Some persons go directly from their house in Lingarajpuram to a brothel in Lingarajpuram; or from Frazer Town to Devajeevanhalli; or from Austin Town to Lingaraj-puram, or from Mathikere to Janata Bazaar; or from Chamraj-pet to Mysore Road, from Jayanagar to Kadikodanahalli from Kanakapura to 9th Block, Jayanagar; from Dodbalpur to Magadi Road, from Bangalore city to Cubbon Park, suburban area, etc.

The persons in the above category can be classified under two headings. One group of persons who come from a rural background, have no education and belong to the lower economic group and mostly 'low' castes. These persons are usually arrested by the police. They do not have money to pay the fine. One of these women said, "The law is for the poor". Even among women, the rich escape by paying a bribe. But a poor person, because she happens to be economically disadvantaged has to face the difficulties and humiliation as a 'women' as well as a 'poor' person. She is doubly exploited.

The second category normally come from 'Backward' communities with some education and knowledge of English. Upper class and 'higher caste' men exploit them. These custo-mers seek their sexual favours but leave them burdened with children, in ill-health, and in a further disadvantaged condition.

Intra-State trafficking in women and children takes place within the state as follows:

Tumkur, Javarayanapallaya village Tumkur to Bangalore; Amanhalli, Belgaum to Bangalore; Belgaum to Sangli Brothel; Village in Indi Road to Gol Gumbaz, Bijapur; Dasayarahalli to Athani, Bijapur; village Nipanu to Saundatti's temple; Darwar to Kammanhalli, Banswadi Hubli to Lingarajpuram; Hubli to Banswadi and Kamanhalli; Puthur to Udipi; Mandhya to Majestic, Bangalore; Karwar to Whitefield; Bagalkot to Siddanor; Basangodi; Hosur, Shimoga, Villages in Bijapur and Karwar to Bellary; K.G.F. (Kolar Gold Fields). Oorgaum and Champion reefs to Lingarajpuram, Bangalore; Nangungudi Taluk Mysore to Mangalore; Ventukuppal Mysore to Bangalore; Mysore to Vankatespuram to Lingarajpuram.

Persons involved in *Inter-State* trafficking are unable to to return the same day. Usually their fathers, husbands, brothers or flesh traders make the necessary arrangements. Many are taken to the hotels. Those who function as call girls get their board and lodging paid by customers. Women and children from illierate and lower economic backgrounds take rooms in hotels on the basis of rent. They come to the city during festivals, horse racing or sports seasons or during the early period of the month, stay for a few days and leave the station. Women who come from villages normally tell their neighbours that they are leaving for their native place or to see a relative who is ill, etc.

With regard to *Inter-State* trafficking the sample shows persons from Tamil Nadu, Andhra Pradesh, Kerala, Bombay, Calcutta and Delhi involved in flesh trade in Karnataka. The trafficking pattern from the different states is as follows:

*Tamil Nadu:-*Mylapore, Madras to Delhi to Hyderabad to Brigade Road Bangalore; Mambalam Madras to Brigade Road Bangalore; Vadapalli, Tamil Nadu to Mambalam to Brigade Road, Bangalore. Madras, Washermanpet to Gurupanapalaya, Bangalore; Madras to Bangalore, Madras to Lingarajpuram, Bangalore. Ooty to Devajeevanhalli; Dinigal to Vanarpet Bangalore; Salem to Ganganahalli; Ghandinagar, Comibatore to Shivajinagar, Bangalore; Tanjavur and Madras City to

Frazer Town, Bangalore, Tamil Nadu to Bangalore Camp, Manvi, Raichur Bistrict.

Andhra Pradesh to Karnataka: Thadepallikuddam near Vijayawada to Guntakal and Bangalore; Vijaywada to Hoshalli, Bangalore; Badvel to Podutunorr to Bangalore; Secunderabad to Bangalore to Agra to Lingarajpuram; Andhra Pradesh to Bangalore Camp, Manvi, Raichur District; Rajamundri to Chickpet, Lodge; village in Guntur to Guntur Town to Chillukalurpet back to village in Guntur to Butkal, Karwar district Karnataka; Nunupalli Andhra Pradesh to Nandiyal to Bellary.

Kerala: Palni to Madras and Madras to Lingarajpuram Banglore.

Bombay to Mangalore to Bangalore. Bombay to Bangalore to Lingarajpuram. Thardev Bombay to Hotel in Bangalore. *Calcutta* to Venkatespuram, Koramangala, Banaswadi and Lingarajpuram.

Apart from persons coming into Karnataka there is a stream going out as per data collected, *viz.*,—Kota Mangalore (girl-running racket) to Bombay; Bijapur to Bombay; Siddhagundepalaya, Madavala to Bombay; Tiptur, Mysore to Bombay; Chamundinagare, Hebbal to Kamatipura, Bombay; Gokak to Bombay brothel; B.D. Quarter Austin Town to Bombay; Austin Town to Lingarajpuram to Bombay; Gurthyappa Colony Shimoga to Bombay brothel; Frazer Town to Cochin, Madras, Calicut and Mangalore. Bangalore to Delhi.

6 KERALA

An analysis of data reveals that there is child prostitution in Kerala. The blind beggars of Thangassery insist their children earn at least Rs. 10 a day, otherwise they are beaten up. There were burnt marks on their bodies. The sample includes a girl of this category who is about 10 years. There is *Inter-State* trafficking in Kerala. Girls from Cochin, Palai and Kottayam, as the data shows, are taken to Bombay, to Karnataka via

Madras and directly to Tamil Nadu respectively. Cabaret
artists are invited from Tamil Nadu and Karnataka for Cabaret
Shows. The sample indicates that the girls from Tamil Nadu
are trained for these shows by dance masters who charge
Rs. 200 for the training. There is evidence of a lady dance
teacher involved in trafficking girls from Palai, Kerala to Tamil
Nadu. The dance performances are held in places such as
Calicut, Cochin, Trivandrum, etc. As the analysis reveals these
girls are sexual exploited.

<h3 style="text-align:center">7 MADHYA PRADESH</h3>

The difficult terrain of dacoit infested Chambal ravines, along
which are situated parts of Agra, Dholpur and Morena,
notorious for flesh trade and gun-running, has helped in
making traffickers prosperous. Poor communication facilities
and lack of roads have also soared up the traffic. And to cap
it all a coterie of politicians who rely on Kanjar and Bedia
votes has also helped taraffickers in a great measure. The
happenings around Dholpur indicate that the trade enjoys the
patronage of officials and politicians. "The trade enjoyed the
patronage of a number of local political leaders. . . . Kanjars,
Bedias along with Gujjars account for over two lakhs of votes
in Dholpur-Bharatpur-Morena Belt." (*Indian Express*, 1.5.84)

An analysis of the data shows there is sexual exploitation
of slum dwellers and little children in Madhya Pradesh. Inter-
State trafficking exists from Rae Bareli Distt. U.P. to Chhatri-
pura village in Morena District of Madhya Pradesh, from Agra
in U.P. to Morena in M.P., from villages in Bankura, West
Bengal to Dholpur in Rajasthan via Madhya Pradesh.

<h3 style="text-align:center">8 RAJASTHAN</h3>

A social science study reveals, PTI reports, that tribal women
carry out prostitution in at least nine villages between Ajmer
and Jaipur, including Dudn, Bandra, Sindri, Dantri, Dausa and
Bagrn.

In Rajasthan truck drivers, travellers, school and college
students, constitute the bulk of the clientele. Girls of the

'Kanjar' and 'Bawari' communities aged between 12 and 20 years are sold at Dholpur, among other places. From Dholpur the girls bought from Madhya Pradesh are then sent to Delhi and Agra for prostitution. . . . Singing and dancing societies have been opened by prostitutes under the Shops and Establishment Act in different localities to carry out prostitution in a clandestine manner. Hotels in Jaipur, Ajmer and Udaipur have separate rooms for these professionals. Often these hotels are frequented by call girls with the connivance of the managements.

There was a rise in cases of teenage prostitution, reported in the study conducted by Dr. Mrs Swarna Lata Hooje in Jaipur. She gave several instances of school girls going in for the trade after school hours. (*The Statesman*, 28.2.84).

9 MAHARASHTRA

The seventies saw a mushrooming of dancing schools in Bombay and the major cities of India. Call girls in the garb of dancing partners and dance teachers used to cater to the sex needs of the middle-aged men at these schools.

Without knowing a single step of dance, they would charge around Rs. 15 for a 45 minute lesson. For 'action' the charges varied from customer to custom er, girl to girl and time to time. Needless to say, the money found its way to the owners of dancing schools, usually a hefty 'dada-type' person who would regularly bribe the police to allow him to carry on the business.

Public outcry saw the phenomenon declining. But the schools closed only to be replaced by massage parlours. Their *modus operandi* is similiar to the one used by dancing schools.

The innocent looking advertisement in the evening dailies read: 'Air-conditoned Health Centre offering superfine massage' or 'Air-conditioned Scientific Health Centre under new address and new management offers simple, electrical battery massage both sides . . .'

Mohan Deep from Bombay in his article on 'Massage Parlours—a big tease' states that during his investigation of this flesh trade in disguise, he was shown the inside cubicle with beds and a seat. A man in his twenties entered and said,

"Powder Masage Rs. 50 oil massage Rs. 60. We also have electric massage."

The researcher included a sample of a girl under the heading "Massage Parlour', Hailing, from a lower-economic level family in Goa, the respondent was on the look-out for a job. She was a teenager and had just completed her High School. A group of persons came to her home town from Bombay to interview girls for jobs. Through her friends she came to know that interviews were being conducted. As she was in need of employment, she approached them. Later she received an appointment order to come to Andheri West Massage Parlour at Bombay. As she hailed from a poor family she had to travel alone from Panjin to Andheri West. She explained to the researcher the life of a girl, what is expected of her, etc., at the Massage Parlour. A present she was in a brothel in Andheri East engaged in prostitution. She had not gone home, she was in a dilemma as to what to do. She sent home money, whatever amount she could. But the family was not aware of her plight.

It is evident from the analysis of samples that sexual exploitation in Maharastra is carried on at local, intra-state and inter-state levels. More data follows:

Girls from local chawls and villages around Bombay are shifted to Foras Road and other parts of the notorious 'red-light' area of Bombay. The victims of sexual exploitation come from Modinagar, D.N. Nagar, Andheri to hotels in Juhu and Commards in Bandra. In Khida Village, Maharashtra, a 16 year old married girl was killed by her husband and in-laws for not offering sexual favours to others. In Kholapur a young woman was raped by a doctor when she went for treatment. A student of Navavodi School was raped after school hours. Some adults were responsible for deceiving her and taking her away from the school.

Intra-State Trafficking in Women and Children

From Kumbalgoan, Sholapur, Malowdi, Thairwadi, Pune, villages of Maharashtra, Raigad District, and Ahmednagar women and girls are either abducted, kidnapped, sold or resold, lured or deceived and bought to Bombay 'red-light' areas for the flesh-trade. Some of the girls from Ahmednagar are also taken to Pune 'red-light' areas.

Inter-State Trafficking in Women and Children: There is inter-state trafficking in women and children from:

(a) Cuddapah, Andhra Pradesh to Kamatipura, Bombay, Hyderabad, Andhra Pradesh to Miraj for the Arabs. Bhimavaram, Vijayawada to Foras Road, Bombay 'red-light' area. Pamanagar, Ongole Jilla District to Bombay brothels. Andhra Pradesh to Pandu Maharaj Chawl, Bombay. Andhra Pradesh to Pune, 'red-light' area.

(b) Panjin, Goa to a Massage Parlour in Bombay West to a Bombay brothel.

(c) Cochin, Kerala to Bombay Hotels and Brothels.

(d) Sonavali, North Delhi to Kamatipura.

(e) Hebbal, Lingarajpuram, B.D. Block Austin Town, to Bombay.

(f) Villages near Hubli, Dharward to Pune.

(g) Tamil Nadu: Girls from Salem, Arakonam are trafficked to Bombay 'red-light' areas *e.g.*, Falkland Road. Some of the girls who were taken to Bombay brothels later shifted to Pune 'red-light' areas.

(h) During field work in Maharashtra the researcher met girls from various states, such as West Bengal.

(i) At one time a group of 18 girls from Mangalore, Karnataka, were interviewed in one brothel, along with their Madam who is also a Mangalorian. The conditions *i.e.* health and facilities extended were better than those in areas like Kamatipura where they were forced to stand on the pavements of the streets.

Being a time-bound study further data collection was not possible in Maharashtra.

10 ORISSA

The recent spurt in the opening of hotels and guest houses has triggered off a thriving call girl racked in Bhubaneswar, city of temples. According to knowledgeable sources, quite a few of the 30 odd hotels, exist because of the clandestine flesh trade.

The number of call girls involved, according to reliable estimates ranges between 150 and 200, mostly in the age group of 15-20 years, 20-25 years and a few above. . . . Whatever be the economic or social strata they represent, the saddest part is that a majority of them are still attending some of the leading educational institutions. Young and educated girls are bought from nearby towns and passed on to prospective clients as students. If one of the 50 odd brokers operating in this city is to be believed, these outstation girls come to Bhubaneswar during college hours everyday by appointment.

The gang of brokers includes a few receptionists, a large number of hotel boys, rickshaw-pullers, a handful of government employees and big contractors.

Cases are also cited where call girls have been made available by a handful of unscrupulous contractors in an attempt to have their project reports or bills approved. (*Times of India* 29.6.84).

While the secondary information has highlighted the existence of call girls in Bhubaneswar, the data in Southern Orissa indicates:

1. *At Local Level*: Women and girls engaged in construction work at Tokipada Village and Koria Valley are subjected to violence and sadistic perversions by male co-employees and contractors. There is evidence of rape and gang rape in Orissa.

2. *Movement from local town and agricultural areas to the 'red-light' areas*: Tribals, sibling of beggars and landless labourers are sent by their families from adjacent Dangrigabad, Jhoripet areas, Nowapode and Hawipet to Nagarampur, 'red-light' area of Jeypore, Orissa.

Women and children from the villages Kadamguda and Gurpet more to Gopalbandu Marg 'red-light' area.

3. *Sale*: Two girls abducted at the 'car' festival, were sold at Vijayanagaram flesh market. One of them was directly sold to Jeypore 'red-light' area, Orissa, whereas the other was first sold to Waltair, Andhra Pradesh, and then to Jeypore 'red-light' area.

These girls had to face torture such as violence, beating, strangling.

4. *Inter-State trafficking* in women and children also exists between Raipur, Madhya Pradesh to the 'red-light' area in Jeypore.

There seems to be two major forms of prostitution in Orissa. One of call girls is in the heart of the City of Bhubaneswar *i.e.*, prostitution in hotels, and the other brothel form of prostitution in the South Orissa—in the 'red-light' areas. There seems to be sexual exploitation at both places at Bhubaneswar and South Orissa by contractors. In a developing state like Orissa, illiterate women and girls from lower economic groups seek employment in construction work. But these women and girls are subjected to sexual exploitation.

11. TAMIL NADU

One of the new forms of Inter-state trafficking in minors of Tamil Nadu is in the form of Cabaret Artistes. A dance master trains young girls in their homes for a sum of Rs. 200. Four dances are taught. Thsee includes a snake dance and a disco dance. When the girl is ready, the agent arrives and takes the girl from her home to other states in India for performance. The agents belong to the organisations situated in Mambalam and Mylapore, Madras. Sometimes the girl's mother or a close relative takes the girl with her to the respective hotel previously arranged for their stay.

Girls from different places, with different languages and religious backgrounds are called for a particular time by the organisation and placed in a hotel, in a metropolitan city. This particular group, who form part of the sample for this study, had 11 girls in their group. These girls are kept busy and under strict supervision, so that it gives them hardly any time to talk to one another, to sleep, to attend to their personal needs, etc. They are taken by taxi to the entertainment areas and brought back. The girls have no way of escaping or tracing their way back in these new cities.

Some of the dances are done scantily dressed. If the police arrest them, the required fine is paid and the same night they give another performance.

After visiting several major cities, such as Palghat, Calicut Ernakulam, Cochin, Trivandram, Kovalam in Kerala; Secunderabad, Guntur, Vijayawada, Rajamundri, Vizag in Andhra Pradesh; Bangalore, Mangalore in Karnataka; Bombay, Nagpur, Delhi, Calcutta, etc., the girls are sent home with an agent. The girls are normally paid Rs. 700 or Rs. 800 a month. Deducting the expenses incurred by way of food, clothing, medicine, etc., the balance is handed over to the family. Some of the girls prefer to send the balance immediately after the receipt of a month's pay.

Girls who come to earn through dance are from the lower economic group. These girls are degraded by the organisation who expect them to come on the stage scantily dressed. The girls are exposed to sexual exploitation by persons who are organising the show as well as by cutomers from outside, either known to or sent by the organisers. One of the girls interviewed joined this group at 12 years. She was raped two months after attainment of puberty. Another girl interviewed took to prostitution at 16. The third girl interviewed just joined the group for the first time. She says all three of them are not aware of STD.

These girls face a lot of insecurity in their profession as Cabaret Artistes, for their services can be terminated if they don't fall in with the demands of the organisers.

During data collection, the researcher heard a mother relate the existence of inter-state trafficking in girls between Tamil Nadu and Bombay 'red-light' area. Her 16 year old daughter worked as a domestic helper. One day she suddenly disappeared.

The girl's parents informed the police. The women said that as the persons involved were close to the politicians, it was difficult for the police to take action. However, the girl was rescued from eunichs, in Bombay, along with about 18 to 19 young girls. While the mother related this in anguish the father of the girl wept bitterly. The girl has contracted V.D.

The researcher once asked a policeman the reason for the existence of a particular 'red-light' area. The policeman replied that some politicians patronise the 'red-light' areas, while others do not. The police are in a dilemma as to what to do.

An analysis of the data shows that at the local level, girls were sexually exploited in Madras city at Central Station (lodges and Ashoknagar), and at Madurai. Girls for National Highway Prostitution are bought by brokers from different parts of Tamil Nadu, sold, resold, etc., as the need may be in the flesh market. Mostly girls from 'Harijan' and 'Scavenger' families are absorbed. Poondamallee to South Arcot has a stream of inter-state trafficking.

Entering Tamil Nadu gives the impression that one is entering a film world. With its huge film posters all over, and film songs, one hears of the existence of prostitution. 'You need to interview some film-stars, film-extras, go to Mambalam; why not go to Mylapore?' these are the words the researcher heard.

The sample includes film-stars who were originally from Kerala and Andhra Pradesh involved in the flesh trade.

There is trafficking in women and children between Nagercoil and Kanyakumari; Tirunelveli, Tuticorin and Thiruchendur; Kerala-Madurai and South Arcot District. Kerala-Cuddalore; Panruti, Cuddalore, Virudachalam and Pondichery, Madurai to Madras, Salem to South Arcot Dist. and Karnataka.

There is inter-state trafficking from Tamil Nadu to Dholpur Rajasthan, Nepal, Kashmir, Delhi, Calcutta, Bihar, Hyderabad Andhra Pradesh, Karnataka, Kerala, Bombay, and Nagpur.

12. UTTAR PRADESH

Data for this study was directly collected from Allahabad, Kanpur and Varanasi. Secondary data was collected from various parts of Uttar Pradesh including Allahabad, Kanpur and Varanasi. Uttar Pradesh has emerged as the hub of the flourishing trade in exporting children to other parts of the country, each fetching to the exporter between Rs. 1,000 and Rs. 2.000.

Knowledgeable sources say that over 10,000 children below 16 are either kidnapped or lured to meet the market demand. According to the police most of the children are from rural areas.

By a strange co-incidence, the industrial capital of the state Kanpur, has been designated by the exporters as their operational headquarters from where the entire traffic is controlled. Over a dozen gangs are said to be operating in the state. Kaval Towns (Kanpur, Allahabad, Varanasi, Agra and Lucknow) are reportedly divided among six gangs.

The children are normally kidnapped from bus stands, railway stations, etc., and once out of their home districts, the gangs take over. These minors are sold from U.P. to Andhra Pradesh, Gujarat, Rajasthan, Maharashtra and Punjab. The official reports said that children were sold in Nepal and Sikkim also.

According to the police sources unintelligent children with good physique are sent with gangs that operate the racket in bonded labour. Children with average intelligence but mischievous are sold to gangs which train them as pickpockets and thieves. Fair complexioned children are, however, introduced into the flesh trade. (*Times of India* 24.3.84).

The analysis of the data collected from Allahabad reveals that only one respondent was involved in prostitution in her own locality, *i.e.*, she moved only from her home in Allahabad to Meerganj 'red-light' area. There was more evidence of intra-state movements, *i.e.*, girls went from Allahabad to Lucknow and back to Allahabad, or from Agra to Allahabad. There was at high incidence of interstate trafficking in persons across state boundaries. Girls from Calcutta in West Bengal, Kolhapur in Maharashtra, Bharatpur in Rajasthan, were found in the 'red light' area of Allahabad. Some had been sold by a circuitous route *e.g.*, from Calcutta to Kanpur to Allahabad, or from Meerut in U.P. to Calcutta to Allahabad.

The data from Varanasi reveals only inter-state trafficking in women and children. No local or intra-state trafficking appeared in the sample. Women from Muzaffarpur, Bhagalpur in Bihar were observed in Maduadech, the 'red-light' area of Varanasi. Nepali girls from Pokhara were sold to Kathmandu and from there to Radhay Shyam's Kotha, Varanasi. Other girls came from Calcutta via Shivadaspur, or from Chintamani, Tamil Nadu via the Foras Road 'red-light' area of Bombay. Still others came from Patna in Bihar via Calcutta in West Bengal.

From Kanpur the data revealed rural to urban trafficking in women and girls, from Sultanpur village to Forlvaligali, Moolganj. One woman had been forced into a brothel by her husband after marriage. Intra-state trafficking was noted from Faizabad to Roliwaligali, Kanpur, and from Deoui to Kanpur via Allahabad.

The data revealed international trafficking from Beerganj and from Rexaul in Nepal to Moolganj 'red-light' area of Kanpur and from Khatmandu to Moolganj, via Gorakpur. Inter-state trafficking was carried on from New Farakka Malda in U.P. to Calcutta in West Bengal and back to Kanpur (Moolganj, 'red light' area).

Apart from the high incidence of trafficking in Allahabad, Varanasi and Lucknow, there is inter-state trafficking carried on in Rae Bareli, Uttar Pradesh, to Morena, Madhya Pradesh; Bangladesh to Delhi through U.P.; Belgharia, West Bengal to Allahabad; Bihar and West Bengal to Dholpur Market in Rajasthan to Uttar Pradesh.

Secondary data reveals that there is multidirectional trafficking in women and children carried on between several states with Uttar Pradesh as the base.

13. West Bengal

Most of the victims of sexual exploitation in this State as emerged from the analysis are from Shonagachi, Abinash Shonagachi; Balpahari; Belpahari Station; Central Calcutta and Industrial Howrah; Porto-para of Kalighat; Prem Chand Boral Street; Panagarh of Burdwan District; Lalbajar-Ratpukur; Parihati; Binpur; Gidur Station; Village Jhargram; village near Silda and from local hotels.

There is movement from villages to Bankura, Lokepur Bankankura.

There is inter-state trafficking between Agra and Shonagachi. One of the victims of sexual exploitation and sale in the sample was orignally from Calcutta. She was sold to a Delhi procurer, he in turn sold her to a pimp in Punjab and he brought her back to Calcutta for flesh trade.

There is inter-national level trafficking in West Bengal as the following reveals:

Young women from poor families in West Bengal seem to be in demand in Uttar Pradesh. According to police sources in Midnapore, women married by Uttar Pradesh boys without dowry are later sold in foreign countries for larger sums, *e.g.*, Amite and Bina got married to youths who demanded no dowry ... but later planned to sell them abroad for Rs. 5000 each through a man in Delhi. (*Statesman*, 5th October 1982). Some of the girls are sold to Arabs in the Gulf (*Sunday* 25th July 1983).

14. Chandigarh

Analysis of data shows that a young woman who had been for medical treatment was raped by medical students.

15. New Delhi

The data reveals that sexual exploitation of women and children is carried on locally in Motibagh, Pushpvihar, Patelnagar, Rajouri Garden, Lakshminagar, Mukerjinagar, Shalimar Bagh, Ramesh Park, Green Park and Kasthuri Garden Marg. There is trafficking in women and children from Kidwai Nagar to a Connaught Place Restaurant to Feroze Shah Road. The data indicates a wide network of inter-state trafficking with Delhi as its centre.

Delhi Inter-State Trafficking

1. Hazanbad, Motihari, Patna Bihar to Delhi.

2. Villages in West Bengal to Delhi.

3. Godavari District and Cuddapah of Andhra Pradesh to Delhi.

4. Tamil Nadu to Delhi.

5. Bangalore, Karnataka to Delhi.

6. Chandiwad Nasik, Maharashtra to Delhi.

7. Sikkandra Mohalla, Agra to Delhi.

8. Kashmir to Delhi.

9. Villages in Nepal to Delhi.

10. Chandigarh to Delhi.

11. Dholpur, Rajasthan to Delhi.

9

SELLERS AND MARKETS

An analysis of the data shows the various flesh triangles, markets of the flesh trade, centres of transit, supply and demand places. It was shocking to find so many of these centres within a short time.

1. Inter-State Flesh Trade Triangles: Transit Centres

The illustrated inter-state flesh-triangles, as the data indicates, function as *transit* centres in the flesh-trade. It is obvious from the illustration that these centres are situated near the boundary of the states. This affords easy transference of women and children from one state to another with the necessary 'natural' protection. These are isolated areas, away from the heart of the city. The abducted, kidnapped persons in this process suffer in a strange environment, with a new language, etc. As a majority of the victims are children, minors, and illiterate they are unable to find their way home.

2. Intra-State Flesh Trade Triangles

Intra-state flesh markets are within the reach of local procurers. These function as supply centres as well. These triangles facilitate internal trade in flesh.

Inter-State Flesh Trade Triangles

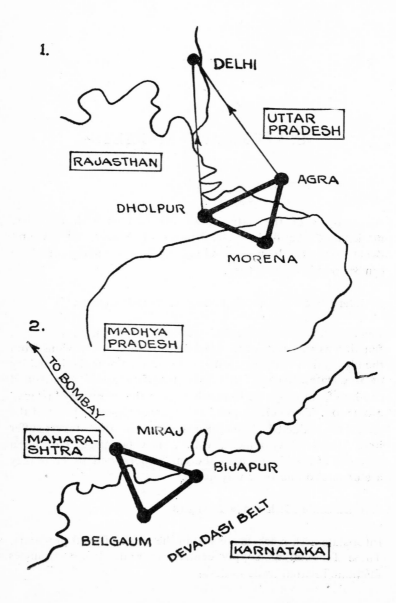

Inter-State and International Flesh Trade Triangles

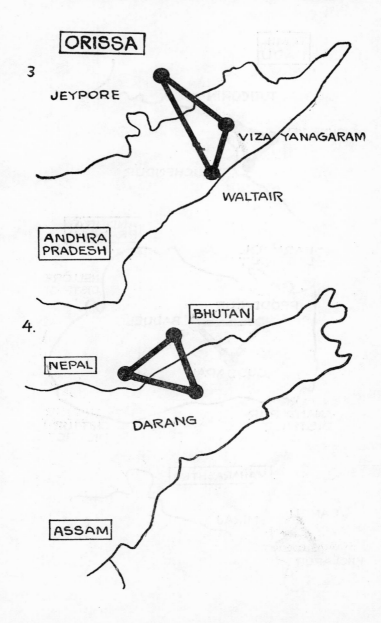

Intra-State Flesh Trade Triangles

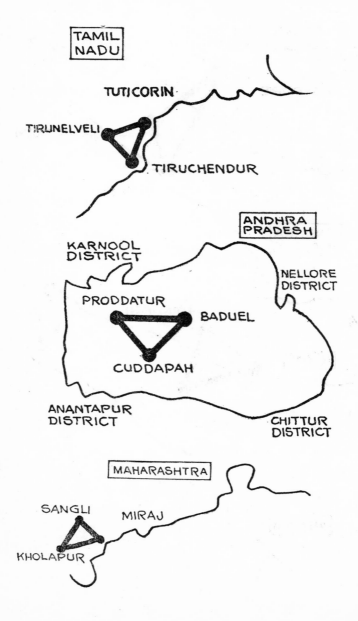

3. Demand, Supply and Transit Centres

Uttar Pradesh in the north and Tamil Nadu in the south function as demand, supply and transit centres.

Varanasi on the banks of the River Ganges in Uttar Pradesh and Madurai with its Meenakshiamman Temple in Tamil Nadu are both religious and tourist centres in India. These places have pilgrims right through the year. On festive occasions these areas are over-crowded. The over-crowding of people, coupled with the easy availability of transport, makes them an easy pitch for flesh traders. There are gangs both in Uttar Pradesh and Tamil Nadu, mainly men, who operate as procurers, brokers, supplers, etc. Women and girls are sold and resold like commodities, for prostitution. The National Highway of Tamil Nadu is called '*Irunda Ullagum*' i e., 'the Dark World'. The Madurai—Madras Highway thrives on the flesh trade. As mentioned earlier a visit to one of these regular spots near Velipuram during the day proved the existence of this flesh trade. Used and a few unused *condoms* were strewn all around the pool.

Trafficking in women and children is carried on between:

Rae Bareli, Uttar Pradesh——Morena, Madhya Pradesh

Patna and West Bengal ——Varanasi, Uttar Pradesh

Rajasthan ——Uttar Pradesh

Howrah ——Shahjahanpur

Bihar and West Bengal } Dholpur, Rajasthan Marher { ——Uttar Pradesh.

Bangladesh——Uttar Pradesh——Delhi

Demand, Supply and Transit Centres

The functioning of some groups of flesh traders as revealed from secondary material is given below to illustrate the enormity of the flesh trade operation in India.

1.   UTTAR PRADESH

Girls are *Procured* from	*Auctioned* at	*Supplied to the*
West Bengal	Biskohar	*Markets* in
Assam	Domariganj	Delhi
Sikkim	Pachperva	Agra
	Itva Bazar	Kanpur
	of Basti Dist	Varanasi
		Lucknow

2.   UTTAR PRADESH

Children *kidnapped*	*Sold* through	*Supplied to*
from several states	gangs from	Andhra Pradesh
	Kanpur	Gujarat
	Allahabad	Karnataka
By KAVAL	Varanasi	Rajasthan
'Exporters'	Agra	Madhya Pradesh
	Lucknow	Nepal
		Punjab
		Maharastra
		Siekkim & Kerala

The Kaval 'Exporters' sell strong and study children for child labour, children with physical and mental handicaps for begging, boot legging, etc., and the good looking ones for flesh trade.

Intra-State Transit Centres are normally situated, as the data reveals, some distance away from the main junction. Bombay, Guntur and Madras have these centres at Kalyan, Vijayawada and Arakonam respectively.

Intra-State Transit

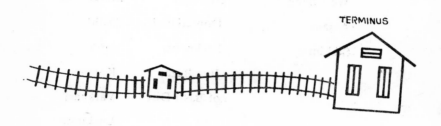

Maharastra	Kalyan	←― ― ―→ Dadar/
	Bombay Central	←― ― ―→ V.T.
Andhra Pradesh	Vijayawada	←― ― ―→ Guntur/
	Hyderabad	←― ― ―→ Secunderabad
Tamil Nadu	Arakonam	←― ― ―→ Madras Central

Demand Centres: Flesh Markets at the National Level

Densely populated Bombay with its urbanisation and industrialisation, with the film-world and entertainment houses, as a centre for tourism, trade and education, is also a city which, through the existence of its vast 'red light' areas, speaks glaringly of the degradation and dehumanization of our Indian women and children.

The massive scale of sexual exploitation and sale of our women and children has made Mr. Amrita Shah rightly call Bombay, "The Great Flesh Bazar" (*Imprint* September 1984). Women and children are trafficked to Bombay from the following states:

Demand Centres

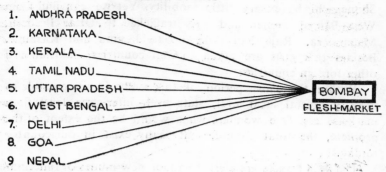

1. ANDHRA PRADESH
2. KARNATAKA
3. KERALA
4. TAMIL NADU
5. UTTAR PRADESH
6. WEST BENGAL
7. DELHI
8. GOA
9 NEPAL

BOMBAY
FLESH-MARKET

Besides Bombay—the gateway of India, Delhi—the capital of India, seems to be the converging point of all trafficking in women and children in India. Like Bombay, Delhi has persons from:

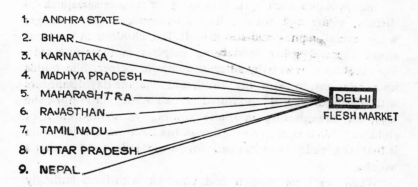

1. ANDHRA STATE
2. BIHAR
3. KARNATAKA
4. MADHYA PRADESH
5. MAHARASHTRA
6. RAJASTHAN
7. TAMIL NADU
8. UTTAR PRADESH
9. NEPAL

DELHI
FLESH MARKET

Delhi, seat of parlimentary and administrative affairs, an abode of politicians and foreign embassies; a centre of tourism and commerce; constant field of national events such as reception of dignitaries and national level sports, etc., a city strewn with posh hotels and centres of entertainment; draws women and children for sexual exploitation from various states of our country. *One of the furthest trafficking is seen from West Bengal.*

Like the Basavis of Adoni, the Surrogate Wives of Shonegachi have very little mobility. Yet we can find from West Bengal women and girls trafficked to Uttar Pradesh, Maharastra, Rajasthan right up to Jammu and Kashmir. Besides this girls are taken to Gulf countries, Pakistan and other foreign countries.

Within the short period of this study it was possible to identify several local level, state-level, inter-state level flesh markets, etc. One wonders what would be the extent of the problem, the total picture, that really exist in our country to-day.

The flesh traders are alert to adopt new modes of functioning. During data collection the researcher interviewed some child-lifters. These persons believe that a child should be kidnapped/abducted as an infant or a toddler. This puts the child in a vulnerable position. The child is unable to explain the situation to others. The child cannot escape, and can be moulded or trained by flesh traders.

Saroja is one such girl. Charming in mannerism, quick to discuss, smart and with a flare for languages, this teenager with several names spots out well fed children in busy bus stops. She offers her services to helpless mothers with kids. She takes up jobs as baby sitter or domestic helper. She builds up a relationship with the child, and one fine day disappears with the child. She is sponsored by an agency in Pimpri, she says, an organisation in Pune dealing with 'adoption of children.' What is most degrading in the flesh-market in India is that the child is bargained for while still in the mother's womb.

When we meet women and children with faces smilingly soliciting customers in the 'red light' areas or at the street corners; or come across fashionably dressed young women standing alone, or rather aloof, at bus-stands and at the road-sides with an air of respectability and reserve—waiting for customers; or see young ladies, smartly dressed with the knowledge of a variety of languages accompanying tourists from five-star hotels, we often conclude from their appearance

and behaviour that these women and children take up prostitution voluntarily. We often rationalise that they adopt a
life of prostitution because of poverty.

An analysis of the data collected gives shocking revelations.
Table 18 gives in a nut-shell the details or categories of persons
responsible for the sexual exploitation of the women and
children in this study.

TABLE 18

**Persons Responsible for the Sexual Exploitation of Women
and Children in India**

Sl. No.	Persons responsible	Frequency	Percentage
1.	Kith and Kin	353	33
2.	Friends and Acquaintances	66	6
3.	Strangers and Benefactors	115	10
4.	Persons involved in flesh-trade	208	19
5.	Persons at the service of society	66	6
6.	Information not available/not applicable	292	26
	Total	1100	100

The above table shows that the highest number of persons
responsible for the sexual exploitation of women and children
is their own 'kith and kin'. This comprises 353 persons, 33 per
cent of the sample. These are the 'loved' persons on whom the
women and children depended trustingly for their survival. A
more specific break up of this group of persons under Kith and
Kin shows they are:

aunt (1); brother (2); brother-in-law (6); brother and purchaser (1); elders *i.e.*, parents and guardians (213); elder sister (1);

father (19); in-laws (1); husband (47); 'husband' (4); husband his two brothers and his mother (4); grand-mother (3); maternal uncle (1); and sisters (2); parents (19); step-mother (1); uncle(2); 'uncle' (3); mother (23).

One often presumes that women and children are sexually exploited only through an organised net-work of gangs, etc., at distant places. It is surprising to see how close and near are persons who sexually exploit our women and children in India.

Another factor that leads women to take up prostitution is what is called *chooth* (leaving). This happens in cases where the marriage has taken place when the couple were infants. When they grow up the couple find they are unmatched for several reasons, and either the boy's family or the girl's wants *chooth* (freedom to leave the other partner). For this, a sum of money has to be paid, especially if the girl wants to leave her husband. She will go with anyone who is willing to pay the *chooth* money and take the girl with them.

Analysis of data indicates that not only kith and kin, but also friends and acquaintances, strangers and the so called 'benefactors' and persons involved in the flesh trade are responsible for this sexual exploitation. These categories of persons involved are:

Friends and Acquaintances: Acquaintances; boy-friends; boy-friend's brother; father's friend; girl friend; future mother-in-law; neighbour; known men and elderly women and parents' enemies. 66 persons (6 per cent) of the sample belong to this category.

115 persons (10 per cent) were strangers and 'benefactors.'

208 persons (19 per cent) were persons involved in the flesh trade. This major group, the second highest in the sample, needs to be spelt out as respondents (who are mostly illiterate and minors) are under their control. Captain F.D. Colabaavala in his book *Sex Slaves of India* (1981) describes these people in a 'red light' areas in India:

'Bombay's 'red light' area is a sensuous and sinister under-world. There are over 50,000 *rundies*, 20,000 *bhadwas*, *yars*, *dadas* and *mawla*. Over 6,000 *ghar.valies*, *goons*, *thugs* and other goondas involved in violence and narcotics, illicit contraband, gambling and 15,000 male prostitutes or hijras with an equal number of their agents with expert knowledge of sexual perversion. They all transact their business openly without fear. But, around the 50,000 ill-fated and often misshapen bodies is built an underworld of the pocket of sin. The world of landlords, gharwallis, and what-have-you-not-got revolves round these 50,000 odd women. It is a world dominated by sex and violence, by drugs and disease.'

Betrayal of love by parents and guardians, deception and deceit from friends and 'benefactors,' traumatic experiences of being kidnapped, abducted, sold and resold by flesh traders, and being forced into prostitution in dehumanizing surroundings makes the women and children give up all hope in society. As a final step these women and children with trust approach the so called persons at the service of society. What is the response? The analysis of Table 20 shows that 66 persons (6 per cent) of the sample were persons at the service of society, who were responsible for sexual exploitation. This group includes businessmen, officials, constables, policemen, contractors of construction work, doctors, medical students, employers, land-lords, lawyers, a manager, military personnel, a minister, MLA, (Minister of Legislative Assembly), organisers of dance troups and music cults, a swami, a teacher, a youth, railway workers, a client (marriage parlour) and a zamindar.

Women and children, sexually exploited and sold, consider the attitude and behaviour of society towards them as an ultimate betrayal of love and rejection. Being born a woman in Indian society is of low status, further the status of a woman who is considered to be a 'prostitute' is much lower; she is ostrasized. She is treated as a non-person, a commodity to satisfy men's sexual needs. Man must be saved from the dreadful disease at all costs. So the female has to be confined to a particular area to get treated.

The condition of our women and children, and what they have to endure is beyond our comprehension. As a society we have failed in our duty towards this section of women and children who are forced to sell their bodies for their livelihood. The degradation of our women and children, paraded on the footpaths and public places by flesh-traders are against human dignity and human rights. Yet the society moves on, unperturbed, undisturbed and some justifying their existence.

10

SUMMARY AND RECOMMENDATIONS

International studies have clearly indicated that prostitution is an universal phenomenon. It has not received priority consideration in many developing countries due to a variety of factors e.g. In the patriarchal set-up of a country where he rulers and law makers are males, problems of utmost urgency, crucial to women are by-passed as secondary. The problem of prostitution is viewed superficially, not in its reality and pushed aside as trivial. Besides, due to the general acceptance of prostitution by society this problem is considered common.

Prostitution is a problem which all societies have to come to terms with, it cannot be ignored. The value any society places on women, the roles attributed to them, their position and status in society are undoubtedly crucial factors in this matter.

International Abolishionist Federation's *Prostitution; Survival of Slavery** states:

"To accept prostitution as a profession (willingly or under duress) is a totally retrograde step depriving women of their independence, privacy and, above all, human dignity, and reducing them to the level of servitude."

*Record of 28th International Congress September 3rd to 6th, 1984. For VII, p.p. 269 & 263.

"Prostitution and the accompanying evil of the traffic in persons for the purpose of prostitution are incompatible with the dignity and worth of the human person and endanger the welfare of the individual, the family and the community."

"............that in all countries in the world prostitution reflects a society in which the domination of men over women and children is perpetuated."

A German doctor, Rudolf Affermann—a psychotherapist and social critic, states, "In the consumer spiritual reactions lead to consumer-reactions, and thereafter for him, love is a matter of consumption. Sexuality is seen as a consumer article and when love has been torn apart from its spiritual context and from the person concerned, it eats away at him, rather in the way an ice-cream is licked away. One's sexual partner is utilized as a consumer article, the partner gets nibbled away. There is manifested a wider need of men or women. One acquires a new friend just as one buys a new fur coat. One transfers to a new girl friend like buying a new car. The consumer combines with others for communal sexual consumption. Nobody wants spiritual relationship, for feelings are awkward. It is easier to get on with sexual consumption if one doesn't have them. Then one can pull out of the situation and turn to a new consumer article."*

Untruthful love and pseudo-relationships, egoism and selfishness, degradation and contempt for women are distortions of reality. In any society, the image of women is consistent with the way men want to see and use them. The sexual act, an expression of mutual love between the marital partners tends to be reduced to an animal operation devoid of tenderness, affection and truthful love.

The consumer in the company of a person who is not his marital partner, engages in sexual activities, enjoys the brutality of sadism, guilt free, as he never has to see the consequences of it.

---

* Quoted by Mr. Hans Arnold Rul (F.R.G.), General Secretary to the International Union for Moral and Social Action—*Prostitution: Survival of Slavery* pg. 35.

What is most alarming is the fact that prostitution now includes still another level of society that has been relatively untouched by the phenomenon until fairly recently—children

Traffic in children is a sphere of crime and consequently of a highly clandestine type. Buying and selling human beings, persons, is forbidden all over the world. Yet, in complete disregard for all human and international laws, the flesh-traders indulge in trafficking children. As this brings in enormous profit, they take tremendous risks, so that the transaction takes place in a highly clandestine situation. Bartering, acceptance of cash is often done in the absence of the victims, their names are changed, they are disfigured and communication barriers are created in various ways.

Lest the victim (child), escaped or rescued, relates his or her origin and family background, the flesh traders adopt innovative methods. e.g. at present, as the data shows, smart adolescent girls, with a knowledge of several languages and a quick wit are engaged in child-lifting. They play with the babes at the bus stops, in railway stations, etc., or offer their services as domestic helpers. At an opportune moment they disappear with the child.

The demographic background of the victims under 'age' reveals shocking evidence of **child prostitution and sexual exploitation of minors in India.**

An analysis of the age of the victims at the time of data collection indicates 384 persons (35 per cent) of the sample as children below 18 years, and 208 persons (19 per cent) as girls between 18 to 21 years. (Table 4)

An analysis of the age of victims at the time of initial sexual exploitation indicates 585 persons (53 per cent) as children below 18 years and 256 persons (23.3 per cent as girls between 18-21 years. (Table 5)

In India only those who have attained 21 years are eligible to vote. Persons below 21 years are deemed as not mature enough to vote. They are considered as minors. **In this light, we have ample evidence of child prostitution** (53 per cent) and sexual exploitation of minors (76.5 per cent) in India.

With regard to the sex of the respondents, 1078 persons (95 per cent) of the sample were females while only 22 persons (2 per cent) were males. Efforts to include more were not possible.

In Indian society, if a woman sells sex, she is considered as a 'prostitute' (receiving cash from a man for sexual favours). If a man sells sex (receives cash from a woman for sexual favours) he is condoned. Even is this case a woman is labelled as a person of weak character, of loose moral standards. The society is greatly influenced by double-standards of sexual morality. As such, women still remain the most exploited section of the Indian community.

In spite of the compulsory education schemes, adult literacy programmes and non-formal education projects launched by the Government of India, 88.2 per cent of the sample remain illiterates. (Table 10) 130 persons have had some form of education. The inclusion of male respondents in the sample has in some measure attributed to the rise in percentage among literates. The need for out-reach programmes in the educational field seems essential.

India being predominantly a Hindu country, most of the victims of the flesh-trade (39 per cent) profess Hinduism. The Muslims and the Christians who comprise the next highest (3.7 per cent & 3.6 per cent respectively,) were converts from Hinduism. (A few were recent converts while in the case of others their parents or grand parents were converts.) Hence some of the concepts, cultures and traditions of Hinduism are imbibed by them. Although all religions uphold the dignity of human beings, persons, in practice, as the study reveals, it is not so. (Table 8)

The victims of the flesh-trade come mostly from castes, designated as Scheduled Castes, and Scheduled Tribes. (Table 9) The caste system introduced for better social organisation and harmonious living, has proved to be an institution of oppression of the 'Lower Castes' by the 'Upper castes'. Great men such as Mahatama Gandhiji, Dr. Ambedkar, etc., made great efforts to eradicate castism in Indian society. Yet, this system prevails. It is obvious that the caste system has an adverse effect on 'Backward' Classes. Most of the victims of the flesh trade who hail from 'lower' castes are economically the deprived sections of our society. Continued efforts for the eradication of the caste system have to be made to provide the the basic needs of every citizen.

In India in all marriages, whether 'arranged' or 'love', an important element of consideration is that the birde-to-be should be a virgin. The birde-grooms moral standards often remain unquestioned. Even if lapses are known, they are overlooked 'after all he is a man', 'one can expect',—this type of rationalisation and justification can can be heard.

Myths, such as 'Sexual relations with virgins cure venereal diseases' makes men, specially customers with sexually transmitted diseases, seek virgins. The demand for virgins, (children and unmarried women) by sadists, paedophiles and persons who indulge in sexual perversions, bring in more virgins to the flesh markets in India.

Of the 172 persons (16 per cent) of the sample who were married (Tables 11) we find various categories of exploitation. Young girls below 15 years have been married to their maternal uncles. (A custom prevalent in some communities in India.) After a couple of years, they face problems of adjustments, or separate, etc. due to the wide age gap. Sometimes the wives are deserted as they have not given dowry at the time of marriage.

Another group of married women in the flesh trade stated that after their marriage, they discovered to their dismay that their husbands were pimps, procurers and flesh-traders. Although initially they had put up a lot of resistance due to various reasons, e.g., no other alternative home or means of livelihood, or no one to help them out, etc., they continued to live with their husbands and comply to their wishes.

Fake marriages in various forms led to some of them being sold to brothels; some were deserted after rape and a few more kept as 'Mistresses'. Marriage racket with the visiting Arabs was also another form of exploitation where the girls, as the data shows, could be divorced on the same day of their marriage. In this context, as a precautionary measure registration of all marriages in India should be made compulsory.

The migratory pattern of the victims of the flesh trade (Table 13) indicates inter-state migration among 326 persons (29.6 per cent) of the sample. 308 persons (28 per cent) the next highest group have had no change except within the vicinity of their place. Inter-State migration is further supported by the Inter-State trafficking in women and children depicted under

Trafficking (Chapter 8). Persons involved in the flesh-trade are alert as to the safe guards to be taken with regard to the identity of the victims and to the demands of the various flesh markets.

To sum up, the demographic background of the victims of the flesh-trade gives us ample evidence of their vulnerability—children, minors, virgins, unmarried women, illiterates, persons of 'Scheduled Castes', 'Scheduled Tribe' Backward Class and deprived sections of the society. In spite of the existing national policies towards protection of women and children, this vulnerable section of the society is exposed to brutality, abuse, multilation, sexual exploitation and sale. Serious efforts have to be made both at local and national level, strategies have to be planned and implemented—as in dealing with the problems of smuggling, drug trafficking, etc.

International assistance has to be sought on the one hand, and on the other, pressure from international levels has to be exerted to eradicate prostitution at national levels.

We have seen in Chapter Five, that the victims of the flesh-trade were sexually exploited in 30 different ways. These were broadly classified under the headings—Prostitution with socio-religious sanctions, traditional forms of prostitution, etc. An analysis of the mode of entry depicts the 735 persons (67 per cent) of the sample have had 33 violent forms of entry (Table 14). Only 124 persons (11 per cent) were lured into prostitution by the flesh-traders. Information was not available with regard to 241 persons (22 per cent).

Besides procuring women and children by illegal and violent means, they are subjected to violent forms of victimization. Chapter 7 (Table 16), reveals 17 ways of subjugating, enslaving the victims. This does not mean that only one form of violence was forced upon them. Often multiple methods were adopted. From branding, whipping, cutting with knives, strangling, gagging, etc. to administerting herbal drinks, drugs, taking photographs, blackmailing, etc.

Rape is a part of almost every sequence of a torture situation. Women and children feel powerless to fight back. The more the resistance the greater the torture. Hence most of the victims find no other way but to comply to the demands of flesh-traders.

Persons belonging to various disciplines such as medical, Police, Social, legal, etc. could do great service to the wounded, mutilated women and children through joint preventive and curative programmes. Crisis intervention centres, reception centres, community vigilance centres scattered in several parts of the villages, towns, cities, of our country can render immediate service to the victims, persons in crisis situations.

What is more degrading in this 20th Century, than to hear of 'price tags' for women and children? Can society sit back and debate whether prostitution needs to be legalised or not while our women and children are bartered and sold for sexual exploitation? What is prostitution—is it not sale of *persons* for sexual exploitation and sale of sex—as *commodities*?

An analysis of the data reveals the highest rate for sale of sex as Rs. 3500 and the lowest as Rs. 2. Sale of persons for sexual exploitation, where the purchaser takes the ownership, complete appropriation of the women's, child's body—the prices vary from Rs. 400 to Rs. 70,000. (Table 17)

A glance at the 'price tags' depicts that the highest price on the index in the flesh-market at present is Rs. 20,000 and Rs. 70,000 for Muslim girls. These girls from West Bengal had originally migrated from Bangladesh and were sold to Jammu & Kashmir. (Rs. 70,000 was for a Muslim graduate, at an auction in Kalyan, Bombay).

The next group that is priced highly in the flesh-market of Delhi and Assam are the tribal girls. The price ranges up to Rs. 46,000 for 4 girls. (Rs. 11,500 each person), Rs. 9000-12,000 for an Assamese girl. Girls from Nepal (special cases) can fetch as high as Rs. 50,000 in Bombay market.

The lowest prices range between Rs. 400 to Rs. 3000 at Bombay V.T.—a girl was sold by her father for Rs. 400. At Arialur, in Tamil Nadu a girl can be obtained for Rs. 400. The same girl can fetch Rs. 1500 at Pondi Market and Rs. 3000 at Bombay Market. The price at Bihar is between Rs. 1000 and Rs. 2000. The foreign market rate for a girl from Kerala was Rs. 60,000.

Whether the price tag is high or low (which depends mostly on appearance, etc.) as persons they all suffer, as victims of the flesh-trade, at various levels, physically, psychologically, mentally and spiritually. Stern action against sale of persons has to be taken. Wide publicity of this evil, should be given. Co-operation of the community has to be given to the police force working on social defence.

Chapter Eight presents state-wise trafficking in women and children. This in-depth study, within a limited time, was able to identify flesh-markets and flesh-triangles, at local, intra-state, levels. The analysis (Chapter 9) further reveals some of the transit, supply and demand centres. Bombay has emerged as the biggest Flesh Bazaar in India (the Gateway of India). This is followed by Delhi (the Capital of India). These places of tourism, commerce, etc. are, as the data reveals, places where the women and children are debased the most. A network of specialized police squads at local, state, regional and national level needs to be introduced to counter-act trafficking in women and children to these demand centres. The existing machinery, at the moment, is inadequate due to limited personnel,compared to the multiplicity and gravity of the present day problems. Enrolment of personnel,both men and women in the police force is essential. Co-operation of the non-governmental organisations and international net-work working on Abolition of Prostitution has to be sought. There is clear indication that the traffic in persons in India moves from south towards north, from east to the west—such as Pakistan and Gulf countries.

At this stage one wonders, who is responsible for this chaos ? Chapter Ten, Table 18, indicates that the first category of persons responsible are the victims' own kith and kin. (33 per cent)

A four year old, raped by her brother's friend who visits their house regularly, a father raping and selling his daughter for prostitution, a mother dedicating the daughter to the goddess while the child is still in her womb, a tribal community forcing their eldest daughters to prostitute for their maintenance etc., continue to be one of the contributing factors for perpetuating prostitution. Mass media could play a vital role in inculcating the worth of individuals, persons; consientizing the public to report exploitations without fear (as silence increases the incidence of sexual exploitation). Programmes on healthy parental care would go a long way in counter-acting exploitation of women and children by their kith and kin.

The next group that is responsible for the sexual exploitation and sale is the 'flesh-traders'. This group often remains invisible. The more key position they hold in the flesh-trade, the more respectable they appear to be outwardly. The researcher met a couple of king-pins during the course of her data collection. These king-pins were immaculately dressed, dignified looking, diplomatic in their manner and well versed in public relations. They seemed to be greatly concerned about the welfare of women and children. Yet, while approaching them, one realises how dangerous these persons can be, one is aware of the serious risks involved—either directly or indirectly. In spite of the risks involved, they have to be approached. Left to themselves, these persons could delve deeper into this evil system of flesh-trade. Yet, they are *persons*, human beings like you and me. They have great potential and if transformed or rather if they transform themselves, they can be great channels of love, peace and development.

Often one hears of *hufta, mamool, kaipidi* etc.—policemen's share—a small bride accepted by some policemen to leave the flesh-traders to carry on this trade uninterrupted. There is a great need for persons who serve the society—policemen, doctors, lawyers, politicians, social workers, educationalists, etc. to be persons of integrity. There are persons, no doubt, who continue to serve the country sincerely. Greater incentives or awards need to be given to police personnel, etc. who unearth flesh-dens, under social defence, as in other cases of theft, smuggling, trafficking in drugs, etc. In our society, women and children need to look up to the persons at the service of the society in various disciplines, for protection, guidance and services, without the fear of being sexually exploited, abused or sold.

As we, as a society, have been responsible for the existence of prostitution in our midst, *so we have a major role in eradicating this dehumanizing evil.* The police force, as custodians and implementers of law have their role. A concerted (both the community and the police) humanitarian, gradual, systematic, persevering, dedicated effort is essential in our struggle against prostitution. In this, as children, as youth and as adults, we have a place and a major role to play.

To conclude, prostitution is one of the outcomes of materialism where the intrinsic worth of individuals, as human beings, persons—is lost. From this study it is evident that India, the land of religions, which was steeped in spirituality is turning materialistic.

Respect for persons is the primary premise of social life and hence the basic principle of social justice. He or she, is a self projected value, an inalienable right, an undestroyable actuality and an irrepeatable possibility. Hence persons cannot be commodified, objectified, sexually exploited, sold. This forms the basis, the fundamental philosophy in our struggle against prostitution.

Towards abolition of prostitution in India, several strategies could be worked out at various levels with links at national and international levels. Here the researcher presents a model. It is my earnest and humble plea that these be implemented, thus ushering in a new society in India where love, peace and development will reign.

A Humanitarian and Community Approach Towards Eradication of Prostitution In India

Prevention	Rescue and Rehabilitation	After Care Service
—'Eradication of Prostitution'—Involvement and active participation of children, youth, adults, organisations of both men and women in drive against prostitution.	—Conscientization and publicity through mass media of the services available towards women in 'red light' areas.	—Genuine concern and acceptance of the victims of flesh trade who are beyond rehabilitation as persons by the society.
—Legislation 'Abolition of Prostitution in India' women's organisation takes the lead (eg. Women's Day Programme).	—Reaching out to persons towards rehabilitation through various services, projects.	—Residential care services to the homeless, destitute.
—'Eradication of Pornography '...'—Youth Movements.	—Identifying, assessing aptitudes, abilities of those rescued, etc, through a network machinery such as used in census data collection towards rehabilitation.	—Opportunities to be provided for preaching their religious beliefs.
—'We need a safe society' 'Children are not for sale'—Children's programmes (e.g. Children's Day Programme).	—Re-education, vocational training and opportunities for education.	—Medical, Psychiatric and counselling services to be extended.

Prevention	Rescue and Rehabilitation	After Care Service
—Use of Mass Media towards conscientization, social change— Programmes on healthy parental care; programmes inclucating human respect, depicting actions taken against prostitution by various groups. Programmes from the government (Social Defence).	—Opportunity to practice religion and yoga.	—Residential care services for the homeless, deserted, and the destitute.
—Introduction and implementation at government level, a network of specialised police squads— local, intra-state, inter-state, national and inter-national—to counter-act trafficking in women and children, flesh-trade.	—Medical, Psychiatric and counselling services to be extended.	—Involvement of children, youth and adults in relief services, recreation services,
—Provision of basic needs to all the citizens of India.	—Institutional care for the homeless.	—Sharing of goods, entertaining aged, sitting by the bed side, listening to those who are worried, are some of the numerous services that can be extended.
—Moral and Religious instruction to be included in the curriculum-school and social life of persons through education.	—Creation of opportunities for providing foster-homes, marriage opportunities.	
—Job opportunities and self-help programmes. Financial assistance to socio-economic program-mes-(social welfare organisations involvement on a massive scale).	—Involvement of a joint, con-certed, persevering effort by governmental and non-governmental agencies.	

Cont.

Prevention	Rescue and Rehabilitation
—Crisis intervention and counselling services to those in crisis situations.	—Extending grant-in-aid to organisations who offer their services in rehabilitation of the victims of flesh-trade.
—Compulsory registration of marriages in India (Women's organisations takes the lead.)	—Acceptance of these persons in society as persons.
—Establishment of local committees for the protection of the vulnerable sections of the society, the deprived sections of the society. (Men take the lead).	
—Creation of healthy recreational centres. Karate for self defence.	

11

CASE HISTORIES

This study took as its sample 1100 cases of sexual exploitation or sale of women and girls from twelve states and two Union Territories in India. In this chapter a few detailed case histories are presented as they were narrated to the researcher. They have been chosen from different states in India to give an all India perspective and to show the pattern of trafficking in girls from one state to another.

1. KARNATAKA

Being born in an affluent family, I had all the material needs one could think of. My father had property in interior Kerala. We had our own house, jewels, etc. But these did not give me peace. There was constant fighting between my parents. My father threatened to cut my mother, to kill her. I ran away from the house to a nearby friend's house.

In my friend's house I worked as a domestic servant. After giving Rs. 50/- to my mother, I saved the rest. In this place I used to meet a dance teacher. She was very friendly. Often she would go on tour. Once she had invited me to join her but I had refused. Later she began inviting me to come and stay with her instead of working as a domestic servant in her friend's house. Seeing how good and kind the teacher was, I agreed to live with her, rather, stay with her. I took my savings, Rs. 600/-

approached my married sister and brother-in-law and saw that my mother was safe with them. Then I left for the dance teacher's house.

The dance teacher, as usual, was busy getting ready for another tour. She told me to come with her. As I had no commitments now, no one to get permission from, I agreed to go with her. There were five other girls besides me and the teacher.

At Thirupathur in Tamil Nadu, I was sold for Rs. 2000 to a Hindu man. He took me to his house. He had his wife and son. This couple said I would make a good match for their son. For a few days they took care of me. Then they began to force me to live with their son as his 'wife'. They promised to settle our marriage soon. I began getting sick of this life. My jewels were taken away on the pretext of getting me medically treated. I was forced by the son to go to other men. I declined...one fine day I heard of the son's marriage. When I saw the bride being brought home, I ran away from that house. With the cash I had on hand I came to Madras and found a domestic servant's job in one of the houses.

While I worked in Madras, a kindly sympathetic young man used to visit that family. He took pity on me. He offered to give me a home. So I left with him, stayed in Madras for a couple of years and left for Bangalore.

At present I am 19 years old. For the past four years I am living in Bangalore. Whenever I need money I go to a brothel in Lingarajpuram. The brothel owner takes 50 per cent of what the customers give me. Today, although born in an affluent family in Kerala, I am languishing in Bangalore, Karnataka, without proper food, clothing and shelter! My health is ruined.

2. UTTAR PRADESH

I belong to a very poor family in Kolhapur rural area, Maharashtra. My father was a farm labourer. At present I am 35 years, I have a wife and two children.

20 years ago, I was working in a 'Swastic Soap Factory' as an unskilled labourer. It was at this time, my father sold my elder sister to a rich procurer and Kotha holder in the 'red light' area at Allahabad—Meergani. I joined this profession about 15 years ago since it is more lucrative. I procure girls from my

village in Kolhapur and nearby areas. 10 years ago the rich man
was thrown out by the land lord with the help of the police. He
left Allahabad.

Now, I don't work on a commission basis. I run a Kotha
independently with the help of my sister. I have so far procured
20 girls for prostitution. I have a prostitute concubine.

But I am not satisfied with my earnings and way of life. My
fellow workers in Swastic Soap Factory earn Rs. 900/- per
month without doing any crime. I have taken to drinking, I am
religious minded. My family deity is Yellamma. Many girls
from my family have been dedicated to Yellamma in the past.

I procure girls generally from village fairs held at the time of
Vijaya Dashmi and Deepawali. As I have been in this profession
for a long time, I am familiar with many procurers of Kolhapur
and nearby districts, so I need not visit many times. Procurers
themselves approach me.

3. DELHI

I grew up in Chandigarh, did my B.A. in Political Science and
came to Delhi to take up a job. Before leaving, my mother said,
'Retain your chastity at all costs'.

In Delhi I just stayed with my girl friend, but soon I met a
young man, accidently and shifted to his place. He was a tele-
phone operator. Our companionship grew into romance and we
began to live intimately. This experience destabilized my archaic
belief system. I headed towards open sex. I learned to enjoy
what is called 'cool-sex' cut off from emotions and the life.

I have given up my early job. At present I stay in *R.K.
Puram* and function as a call girl. The agents fetch customers.
I earn two to three thousands a month, sufficient to meet my
requirements.

4. MAHARASHTRA

I was born in Maharashtra. When I was three years old my
father died. My elder brother and younger sister are married
and live with their families. My elder married sister died. At
present my mother, unmarried brother and myself live together.

Although we are only three members in the family, there is no happiness. My unmarried brother either sits at home idle or roams around the city with his friends. My mother forces me to get married. She hates to see my boy friend come home. My boy friend asked me to marry him. I am not inclined to do so. My mother is an alcoholic. She drinks 'Saraya'—cheap liquor, local made stuff and beats me up. When she is sober she enquires the reason for the wounds on my body.

In Raichur District, Karnataka, I was accused of child-lifting of a five year old boy.

Well,—Yes, I know of a place in *Punpri*, near Poona, where an agency is involved in child-lifting. It has adoption services too. There are about 14 to 30 girls, and 4 to 5 children at the moment. They meet near Ashok Talkies. This is a big market place. Children are sent to foreign countries.

In the past, flesh-traders needed young girls, women etc. Now the trend is toddlers, kids. These can be trained. Besides there is no danger of giving away their background or details once they escape or are rescued.

I am 16 years old, normally young smart girls are selected for child-lifting. These girls are seen near bus-stands, railway stations. They look for healthy, good looking babies. They pose as gentle, kind hearted helpers. They build up friendship with children and their mothers. If they entrust their children, they disappear with them. If not, they ask for a job as domestic helper. During their service, at an opportune moment, they carry away the child......Yes, I had skin infection, when I came. Was it V. D?, Well, I don' t know, I had been treated for it.

5. ANDHRA PRADESH

21 years ago I was born in Badwel,Andhra Prabesh, and lived in Washwerpet. I came from a Muslim family. My father was a fruit merchant. When I was 3 months old my mother died. My elder brother and sister are married and live in Proddatur.

My father re-married after my mother's death and has three children by my step-mother. Both my father and mother do not care for me. My father wanted me to marry an old rich man—that was 10 years ago when I just grew up—(I was about 12 years). I went away to my married sister's place and remained there for 2 years. But how long can one stay in a married sister's house? I returned home. Although I felt unwelcome in my house, I continued staying there till the age of 16 when I meet a rich Muslim woman at the cinema theatre. She looked like an officer with whom one can confide, seek help. So I opened my heart to her. She at once said, "I have all sons. I always wanted a girl." So she took me to her home and looked after me well for six days. She had all sons—big and small.

On the sixth day she took me to *Proddatur* and left me with Bhogamma. I thought Bhogamma was a friend of my 'benefactor'. But later I came to know that I was sold for Rs. 5000.

In Bhogamma's house there were 5 girls. I was forced—after torture—to take to prostitution. I have to be available for customers from 10 a.m., to 10 p.m. 5 to 10 customers per day. Being the youngest in the group I was on demand. One day, my luck, the police raided the place. I was rescued.

6. UTTAR PRADESH

I have done Intermediate. My job is sale of girls to Nayika in the *red light area of Kanpur-Moolganj*. I procure the girls from Uttar Pradesh, Madhya Pradesh and Nepal. They are easily available in Nepal. There is no need to cheat them. Poverty is so pressing in some areas of Nepal, even parents sell their small girls between 8-14 years, for the purpose of prostitution. Some times girls join us due to low morality and less job opportunity.

I am involved in this business since this is more paying than any other service. I earn Rs. 3000 to Rs 4000 a month. It is a profession like any other. So far I have sold 12 girls in Moolganj.

My relationship with the local politicians is good, they help and patronize them. There is no need even to bribe the police.

7. BIHAR

(a) I was born in Purole Region of Tehri-Garhwal. We belong to a Harijan Caste. My father worked in bondage to the village landlord. He had taken from the village landlord loans for my two elder sisters' marriages. Both my poor parents were grateful for his assistance. Now my sisters are living with their in-laws.

After my sisters' marriage only four of us lived in that village. My father, mother, paralysed brother and myself. Besides our meagre income, we had heavy debts to pay. The landlord who advanced loans to my father appeared to be sympathetic and came to rescue my father. He said, "I know a man who can marry your daughter on bride price of two thousand rupees from which you can clear off your debt". It was something that my father had to accept. This is how I got married.

Having married me, I was taken to Delhi and sold. From Delhi the purchaser re-sold me to this place- *the red light area in Muzaffarpur, Chaturbhujistan.*

(b) My father was a landless tribal. I used to help my father in his work. When I was twenty years old I met another tribal girl about 23 years old who had been earlier helping her father in his work in the fields. We were from adjacent villages— Damgrigandad, Jhoripet.

The 23 year old tribal girl gave up her agricultural work and took to prostitution. She earned more than Rs. 100 a week. So I left my work and joined her. We both now stay in *the red light area, Nagarampur.* We have rented a room. Our charges are higher than the Raipur rate (Rs 10). We have had the experience of being beaten up, strangled or locked in a room.

KARNATAKA

12-year old Kesari hails from a village in Guntur District, Andhra Pradesh. She completed her education up to Std V in her own native village school. She was sent to another village to do her higher studies along with a group of village girls. At the time of the mishap she was studying in Std VII.

A teenager in her school was very kind and friendly. She told Kesari that her parents lived in Guntur. She was staying with her relatives near the school. She had invited Kesari to her parents' house in Guntur several times. Kesari declined her invitations. But one day, her friend told her it was a matter of only five minutes by bus and she could return fast— so Kesari agreed to go with her.

The bus heading for Guntur stopped at the busy bus stand at Guntur. Along with the others Kesari got up from her seat and got down with the others. To her dismay she found her friend was missing. Kesari searched all over for her friend, but could not find her. She felt lost and began to cry.

A milk vendor approached her and offered to help her out. She invited her to a nearby house and offered her some food and drink. Kesari was not in a mood to eat or drink. She refused. But the woman insisted that she at least take the drink. In order to get going soon, Kesari drank the 'green' drink. She felt a sort of 'numbness' creeping all over her mouth and throat. The milk vendor took her to Guntur bus stand and made her get in to another bus. Kesari found that this bus was not her village bus. She refused to get into the bus. The woman forced her into the bus. Kesari began to shout and scream. She found that she had lost her speech. She began to gesticulate. The people in the bus made enquires to which the woman answered that Kesari was a dumb girl, a very adamant one too! So no one bothered to help her out.

Kesari was taken to Chillukalurpetta and sold to a brothel owner. In this place there were several huts with many girls. Kesari was told to put on the clothes and cheap ornaments given by them and stand at the entrance of the hut and solicit customers. Kesari refused to do so. She was beaten up, starved, locked up in a dark room. As she did not comply, men were sent to rape her. Kesari had not attained puberty when she was sexually exploited and sold. From then on she was forced into prostitution.

One day when the brothel owner had taken her to a lodge for prostitution, she met her father who had been looking for her all over. He grabbed Kesari from the brothel owner's hand. But the iron grip of the flesh trader was too strong! After argument, it was decided (a) that her father pay the brothel owner a big sum of money within a specified time, (b) that whatever money he had at the moment be handed over to the brothel owner, (c) that the whole matter be treated confidentially lest dire consequences follow.

Kesari was happy to be back home. She was told to discontinue her studies. One day while she was watching the village children at play, she was lifted up suddenly and thrown into a passing lorry. There were some masked men in the lorry. The lorry sped to a far off distant land. During this journey Kesari found that one of the masked men was the brothel owner from Chillukalurpetta. She was brought from Andhra Pradesh to Karnataka. Kesari was sold to a big brothel owner at Bhatkal (a coastal town).

Arrangements for her to be sent abroad were going on. Kesari was looking for some way of escape. At last with the help of a sympathetic woman, she escaped from the brothel. She ran for her life. When she came to the station, she could not get into a train as she had no ticket. For a moment she hestitated and looked back. Lo and behold, a couple from the big brothel were heading for her. Kesari rushed to the nearby police man and caught hold of his feet. She begged him not to send her with these people. Kesari was given protection.

Today Kesari's troubles are still not over. Her own father has lost his mind. He is unable to recognise her, Kesari had no mother. Her father was to her a father and a mother. "Who will take me home?" asks Kesari. No one will, for they are afraid of the flesh traders. "Is there no place for me in society?" she asks!

In Indian society, fear of the flesh traders keeps many a family from reporting such incidents. The presence of a girl who has been forced into prostitution is unwelcome. So even if the family comes to know of the whereabouts of the child, they prefer, as a family told me, "that god takes her". i.e., they prefer her to be dead than come home!

Kesari's life experience, as shared by her, gives us a clear picture of the workings of the underworld. Luring, use of herbal drink, sale, torture, forced into prostitution, releasing the girl under various conditions, abductions by masked men, inter-state traffic, resale. The broken persons—father and child—a child without a home.

Trafficking Pattern:

An analysis of this case history shows that Kesari hails from:

1. A *village* in Guntur District. Lured to Guntur town by a teenage girl. *Guntur is a Transit Centre at State level.*
2. Guntur town (busy bus stand). She is sold to a brothel owner in Chillukalurpetta by a woman (milk vendor). *Chillukalurpetta is a local flesh Market. A Transit Centre at Inter-State level.*
3. Kesari is abducted and resold at Bhatkal coastal town in Karnataka. *Bhatkal is a flesh Market. A supply Centre at Inter-national level.*
4. Arrangements were being made to send her abroad. The brothel owner of this big brothel has been described by the girl as a Muslim. Was she going to be sent to Gulf countries? We are not sure. What is certain from the girl's account of her experience is *that the demand centre is overseas.*

BIBLIOGRAPHY

BOOKS

Bernard Haring CSSR *Free and Faithful in Christ* Volume 2.
The truth will set you free. Middlegreen, Slough SL3 6BT
St. Paul Publications, 1979.

Biswanath Joardar *Prostitution in Historical and Modern Perspectives*—New Delhi Inter India Publication, 1984.

Captain F.D. Colabaavala *Sex Slaves of India,* Bombay, 1981.

Jean Vanier *Man and Woman He Made Them* the first Indian
Edition—Arranged with Darton, Longman and Todd Ltd.
89, Lillie Road, London, SW6, IUD.
—Printed in St. Paul Press, Bangalore-73 Published by the
Bombay St. Paul Society, 1985.

Kathleen Barry *Female Sexual Slavery U.S.A.* Discus Printing,
March 1981.

Mumtaz Ali Khan *Seven Years of Change* A Study of some
scheduled castes in Bangalore, District.
Published for the Christian Institute for the Study of Religion
and Society, Bangalore by the Christian Literature Society,
Madras 1979.

Rosemary Radford Ruether *Sexism and God Talk* Professor of
Applied Theology at the Garrett—Evangelical Theological
Seminary in Evanston, Illonois. Published by SCM Press Ltd.
26-30 Tottenham Road, London. NI. 1983.

S.K. Ghosh *Women in a Changing Society*, New Delhi, 1984.

Stella Faria, Anna Vareed Alexander, Jessie B. Tellis-Nayak *The
Emerging Christian Woman* WINA, Bangalore. Satprakashan
Isvani, Sat Prachar Press, Indore 1984.

The Geeta

The Holy Bible

The Quran

Ashok Mitra ICSSR *The Status of Women's Literacy and Employment,* Allied Publishers, New Delhi.

A Statistical Profile *Women in India,* Government of India, Dept. of Social Welfare, New Delhi.

Fr. Joseph Velam Kunnel *Liberation of Women,* CRI Patna Unit Article 'The Christian Response to the Exploitation of Women,.

Simone de Beauvoir *The Second Sex.*

Suthinee Santaputra "Problem of Impoverished Women Migrants in Bangkok Metropolis", in *Women in Development.*

REPORTS / POLICIES / PAPERS / PAMPHLETS

Anima Basak *Prostitution: Survival of Slavery* Record of the 28th International Congress held at the Vienna International Centre, September 3-6, 1984.

The International Abolitionist Federation with the United Nations Centre for Social Development and Humanitarian Affairs and with the support of the Government of Austria.

Dr. J.V. Jeyasingh *Children in Prostitution:* Papers presented at the seminar on "Women and Crime", Vellore, March 1984.

Government of India *National Policy For Children* Ministry of Social Welfare, New Delhi—22nd August 1974. Printed at Akashdeep Printers, 20 Daryaganj, New Delhi-110002.

Kathleen Barry, Charlotte Bunch, Shirley Castley (edited) *International Feminism: Networking Against Sexual Slavery* Report of the Global Feminist Workshop to Organise against Traffic in Women. Rotterdam, the Netherlands. April 6-15, 1983.

K.D. Sikka *Sale of Sex:* Indian Perspectives and Realities. Department of Criminology and Correctional Administration. Tata Institute of Social Sciences, Deonar. 22 September, 1983.

Shanker Patil M.A. *Devadasi System: Problems and Perspectives* Former Editor—Carmveer. No place of printing and date.

S.P. Punalekar *Prostitution in India* Immorality or Social Subjugation? Legal Education and Aid Society. Documentation Service. For Private Circulation Only. 15th April & 1st May, 1985.

MAGAZINES, PERIODICALS AND BULLETINS

Banhi An occasional journal of the Joint Women's Programme, Bangalore, India. Published by the Honorary Director, William Carey Study and Research Centre, Calcutta, Printed at Printers India, Bangalore-42.

Eve's Weekly Published by B.C. Venkatesh for The Proprietors of Eve's Weekly Ltd., J.K. Somani Building, Bombay Samachar Marg-23 and Printed by him at Sanj Vartaman Press, Sewri, Bombay-15.

Magazine, *'FOR YOU'* Fortnightly. Article—'Buying and Selling of Indian Women.

Imprint Business Press Monthly Publication—Surya Mahal, 5 Burjorji Bharucha Marg, Bombay-23, India.
Distributed by India Book House.

India Today A complete news magazine Editorial office Living Media India Pvt. Ltd. F-40 Connaught Place, New Delhi-1. General Manager Chander Rai, Editor Aroon Purie.

Manushi A journal about women and society, New Delhi-24. Printed, published and edited by Madhu Kishwar on behalf of Mahushi Trust at Everest Press, Delhi-6.

Religion and Society Bulletin of the Christian Institute for the Study of Religion and Society. P.O. Box 4600, 17, Miller's Road, Bangalore-46.

The Illustrated Weekly of India The feature magazine printed and published for the proprietors, Bennett, Coleman and Co. Ltd. by Pritish Nandy at the Times of India Press, Dr. D.N. Road, Bombay-1.

NEWSPAPERS AND MAGAZINE SECTIONS

1. Daily (Jubalpur M.P.)
2. Deccan Herald

3. Express Magazine
4. Express News Service (Mysore)
5. Hindu
6. Hindustan Times
7. Indian Express
8. North India Pathrika
9. Patriot
10. Statesman
11. Sunday (Orissa)
12. Sunday Herald
13. Sunday Statesman
14. Thina Thanthi (Tamil Nadu)
15. The Times
16. The Times of Deccan
17. The Times of India News Service (Srinagar)

RE-DEDICATION

To humanize not dehumanize,
To value not debase,
To liberate not enslave,
To build not destroy
To love and cherish,
Not exploit and sell
The women and children of India.

SOME OF OUR OUT STANDING PUBLICATIONS

BIOGRAPHIES

Balasubramanian, M.	Nehru: A Study in Secularism.	45.00
Hussan, Riaz	Iqbal: Poet and his Politics	125.00
Malik, Inder Lal	Dalai Lamas of Tibet	90.00
Rawlinson, H.G.	Shivaji the Maratha: his Life and Time	75.00
Sandhu, A.S.	General Hari Singh Nalwa: Builder of the Sikh Empire.	125.00
Sharma, O.P.	Great Men of India.	150.00

ECONOMICS

Barman, Kiran	Public Debt Management in India	150.00
Bhargava, P.K.	Essays on Indian Economic Planning.	90.00
Bhargava, P.K.	Some Aspects of Indian Public Finances.	125.00
Centre for Policy Research, N. Delhi	Population, Poverty and Hope.	300.00
Handa, K.L.	Programme Performance Budgeting	75.00
Jain, Anil Kumar	Some Aspects of Income-Tax Administration in India	100.00
Jain, D.K.	Project Planning and Appraisal in Planned Economy: The Indian Context	75.00
Kamble, N.D.	Bonded Labour in India	60.00
Kamble, N.D.	Migrants in Indian Metropolis.	75.00
Kedia, Kusum Lata	Local Finance in an Indian State: Municipal Finance of Varanasi Division Since 1951.	200.00

Rastogi, P.N.	India 1981-86: A forecaste on Economic, Political and Social Developments.	50.00
Khanna, Rita	Agricultural Mechanisation and Social Change in India	125.00
Shrivastava, M.P.	Problems of Accountability of Public Enterprises in India	250.00
Roy, R.C., *IAS*	State Public Enterprise in India.	200.00
Wishwakarama, R.K.	Urban and Regional Planning Policy in India.	75.00

EDUCATION

Bayti, Jamnalal	Problem of Education in the third world.	200.00
Bayti, Jamnalal	Readings in Education.	150.00
Paliwal, M.R.	Differential Effectiveness of Micro-learning.	50.00
Paliwal, M.R.	Social Change and Education.	175.00
Paliwal, M.R.	The Teacher Education on the Move: Today and Tomorrow.	225.00

HISTORY

Anderson, G. & Subedar, M.	The Expansion of British India (1818-1858).	150.00
Aspinall, A.	Cornwallis in Bengal.	200.00
Biswas, Atreyi	Political, Social and Cultural History of Ancient India (H).	125.00
May, L.S.	The Evolution of Indo-Muslim Thought from 1857 to Present.	350.00
Madan, J.C	Indian Police.	110.00
Mohanta, Bijan	Administrative Development of Arunachal Pradesh 1875-1975.	150.00

| Rawlinson, H.G. | Indian Historical Studies. | 200.00 |
| Sikka, R.P. | The Civil Service in India. | 150.00 |

LAW

Ahangar, Mohd. Altaf Hussain	Customary Succession Among Muslims.	175.00
Chaudhari, R.L.	The Concept of Secularism in Indian Constitution	150.00
Jagannadham, V.	Administration and Social Change.	60.00
Saksena, H.S.	Safeguards for Scheduled Castes and Tribes: Founding Father's View.	200.00
Singh, S.S.	Administration of Natural Justice in India.	250.00

LIBRARY SCIENCE

| Pandey, S.K. Sharma | Dewey Decimal Classification for Indology. | 200.00 |
| Rajjan Lal and Kidwai, Nasira | Practical Cataloguing Procedure (Hindi). | 95.00 |

POLITICAL SCIENCE

Baruah, A.K.	System Analysis in Political Science: A Marxit Critique of David Easton.	125.00
Chaudhari, R.L.	The Concept of Secularism in Indian Constitution.	150.00
Gabriel, Soloman	Foreign Policy of Canada	95.00
Ghosh, Partha S.	Sino-Soviet Relations: U.S. Perception and Policy Resp.	100.00
Kaushik, S.N.	Pakistan under Bhutto's Leadership.	175.00
Mahendra Singh	Indo-U.S. Relations: A Political Study.	75.00

Mishra, Upendra	Caste and Politics in India.	225.00
Mukarji, Nirmal and Ashis Banerjee	Democracy Federalism and the future of Indias Unity	60.00
Pai Panandiker, V.A. and Arun Sud.	Changing Political Representation in India	65.00
Pal, J.J.	Jinnah and the Creation of Pakistan.	75.00
Pandey, Jawaharlal	State Politics in India.	90.00
Pillai, G. Narayana	Social Background of Political Leadership in India	90.00
Pirzada, Syed Sharifuddin	Evolution of Pakistan	275.00
Rao, V. Bhaskara	General Elections in India.	200.00
Reddy, P. Ranjani	The Role of Dominant Caste in Indian Politics.	125.00
Seshadri, K.	Studies in Indian Polity.	150.00
Seshadri, K.	Studies in the problems the third world.	175.00
Sharma, T.R.	New Challenges in Indian Politics.	175.00
Singh, L.P. *ICS*	Electoral Reform: Problems Suggested Solutions.	95.00
Singh, L.P.	India's Foreign Policy	55 00
Singh, S.P.	Perspectives in Indian Politics and Administration.	60.00
Verma, S.P.	Indian Parliamentarians: A Study of the Socio-Political Background.	90.00
Vijay Kumar	Indian and Srilanka-China Relations 1948-84.	125.00

PUBLIC ADMINISTRATION

Banerjea, Pramathanath	Public Administration in Ancient India.	125.00

Bawa, Noorjahan	People's Participation Development Adm. in India	125.00
Bhattacharjee, Debasish	Bureacracy and Development in Meghalaya.	150.00
Bhattacharya, Mohit	Bureaucracy and Development Administration.	50.00
Bhattacharya, Mohit	Management of Urban Government in India	50.00
Bijan Mohanta	Administrative Development of Arunachal Pradesh, 1875-1975.	150.00
Dey, Bata K.	Bureaucracy Development and Public Management in India.	80.00
Jagannadham, V.	Administration and Social Change.	60.00
Jain, R.B. and P.N. Chaudhuri	Bureaucratic Values in Development.	120.00
Jain, R.B.	Comperative Legislative Behaviour.	50.00
Padhi, A.P. and Mishra, S.N.	State Administration in India (in 2 Vols.)	350.00
Panda, Basudev	Indian Bureaucracy: An Inside Story.	60.00
Partap Singh	Urban Government in India	45.00
Rai, Haridwar and S.P. Singh	Current Ideas and Issues in Indian Administration	70.00
Sharma, P.D.	Police and Criminal Justice Administration in India.	125.00
Sharma, P.D.	Police, Polity and People in India.	125.00
Sikka, R.P.	The Civil Service in India.	150.00
Singh, L.P. ICS	Sadar Patel and Indian Administration.	25.00
Singh, S.S.	Administration of Natural Justice in India.	250.00

Sundeep Khanna, *IAS*	Civil Administration in India.	60.00
Trivedi, B.V.	Prison Administration in India: Model Prison Programme.	120.00
Wishwakarma, R.K.	Urban and Regional Planning Policy in India.	75.00

SOCIOLOGY

Ahangar, Mohd. Altaf Hussain	Customary Succession Among Muslims.	175.00
Amir Hussain, *IAS*	A tribe in Turmoil: Socio-Economic Study of Jammu Gujars of Uttar Pradesh.	150.00
Brett-Crowther, M.R.	Brandt, Bread and the Bomb: Reflexions on the World Problematic.	90.00
Bawa, Noor Jahan	People's Participation Development Administration in India	125.00
Centre for Policy Research, N. Delhi	Population, Poverty and hope.	300.00
Chaudhari, R.L.	The Concept of Secularism in Indian Constitution.	150.00
Durrany, K.S.	Religion in Society.	200.00
Ghosh, Subhra	Female Criminals in India.	125.00
Jagannadham, V.	Administration and Social Change.	60.00
Kamble, N.D.	Bonded Labour in India	60.00
Kamble, N.D.	Migrants in Indian Metropolis.	75.00
Khan, Mumtaz Ali	Scheduled Caste and their Status in India.	75.00
Khan, Mumtaz Ali	Status of Rural Women in India.	75.00
Khan, Mumtaz Ali	Social Legislation and the Rural Poor.	50.00
Khan, Mumtaz Ali	Muslims in the Process of Rural Development in India.	150.00

Krishnakumari, N.S.	Status of Single Women in India.	125.00
Mandal, B.B.	Tribals at the Polls: A Study of Khunti in Chotanagpur.	90.00
Madan, J.C.	Indian Police.	110.00
Menon, M. Indu	Status of Muslim Women in India.	50.00
Mishra, Upendra	Caste and Politics in India	225.00
Mishra, S.N. and Kushal Sharma	Problems and Prospects of Rural Development in India.	80.00
Mohan, N. Shantha	Status of Nurses in India.	60.00
Paliwal, M.R.	Social Change and Education.	175.00
Pai Panandikar, V.A. and Ajay K. Mehra	People's Participation in Family Planning	160.00
Pai Panandiker, V.A., R.N. Bisnnoi and O.P. Sharma	Organisational Policy for Family Planning.	125.00
Pai Panandiker, V.A. and P.N. Chaudhuri	Demographic Transition in Goa and its Policy Implications.	40.00
Pandey, K.K.	Rural Development in India: Continuity and Change.	125.00
Pillai, G. Narayana	Social Background of Political Leadership in India.	90.00
Rajgopal, P.R.	Communal Violence in India.	140.00
Rastogi, P.N.	India 1981-86: A forecaste on Economic, Political and Social Developments.	50.00
Ray, B. Datta	The Emergence and Role of Middle Class in North East India.	100.00
Ray, B. Datta	The Pattern and Problems of Population in North-East India	250.00
Rita Khanna	Agricultural Mechanisation and Social Change in India	125.00

Rita Rozario	Trafficking in Women and Children in India	125
Saksena, H.S.	Safeguards for Scheduled Castes and Tribes: Founding Father's View.	200.00
Seshadri, K.	Studies in Indian Polity.	150.00
Seshadri, K.	Studies in the Problems of the Third World.	175.00
Sharma, P.D.	Police and Criminal Justice Administration in India.	125.00
Sharma, P.D.	Police, Polity and People in India.	125.00
Sharma, R.N. & Santosh Bakshi	Tribes and Tribal Development: Select Bibliography.	250.00
Sinha, R.P.	Social Dimensions of Trade Unionism in India.	90.00
Singh, K.P.	Tribal Development in India	250.00
Singh, S.S.	Administration of Natural Justice in India	250.00
Singh, S.S. and S. Sundram	Emerging Harijan Elite: A Study of their Identy.	125.00
Trivedi, B.V.	Prison Administration in India.	120.00
Wishwakarma, R.K.	Urban and Regional Planning Policy in India.	75.00

REFERENCE BOOK

Desmukh, C.D.	Amarakosa: Gems from the Treasure House of Sanskrit Words.	90.00
Durrany, K.S.	Religions in Society: Select Indian Press Index of Comparative Religion.	200.00
Pandey, S.K. Sharma	Dewey Decimal Classification for Indology	200.00
Sharma, R.N. and Santosh Bakshi	Tribes and Tribal Development: Select Bibliography.	250.00